Rich Bride
Poor Bride

Your Ultimate Wedding Planning Guide

RichBride PoorBride

WILEY

A Lark Production / John Wiley & Sons Canada, Ltd.

To Jennifer…with a kiss we began
our wondrous journey

CONTENTS

chapter one

In the BEGINNING

chapter two

Get Down with YOUR BUDGET

chapter three

Va-va-voom YOUR VENUE

"I do, but at what cost?"

Your wedding is not only a symbol of your love, it is the best excuse you'll ever have to throw a fantastic party. Wedding planning is also the one time in your life when everyone and everything will emerge from the woodwork—giant hopes, total despair, endless parental advice, long lost (and better off forgotten) friends, sudden-onset color-swatch anxiety, and the scariest of all: budget fears. Don't worry! With a little expert help, the couples from *Rich Bride Poor Bride* all survive their wedding planning and thrive on their wedding day. Throughout the following pages you'll see how you, too, can turn wedding day dreams into reality. On any budget.

And with this book, you've now got all our planners in your back pocket! Drawing on the literally hundreds of requests made of them throughout their careers, the *Rich Bride Poor Bride* wedding planners turn seemingly impossible wedding dilemmas into one creative solution after another. It's no surprise that *Rich Bride Poor Bride* is now being watched in over 70 countries around the globe: spouses-to-be everywhere are looking for real tips on how to do weddings their way without breaking the bank.

For fans of the show and for all new couples about to embark on planning a truly memorable day, this guide is about you as a couple not giving up your vision. Everything you need to plan your day on your budget is here.

—Sean Buckley
Author
Creator, *Rich Bride Poor Bride*
www.buckproductions.com

Acknowledgments

It takes many hands to make a successful book, and I would like to send out special thanks to our incredible, enthusiastic team for all of their efforts.

Rich Bride Poor Bride is currently airing in over 70 markets around the world, and we'd like to thank all our broadcast partners including Alliance Atlantis Communications, Slice™ and Women's Entertainment Network (WE tv), not to mention some exceptional individuals: Vanessa Case, Lisa Godfrey, Nataline Rodrigues, Amy Waters, and Solange Bernard, all of whom have embraced the concept of the show and trusted Buck Productions to bring it to fruition. Also Kim Martin, Elizabeth Dorée, Gary Pipa, and Harold Gronenthal from WE tv, who ran with our vision to air *Rich Bride Poor Bride* to audiences in the United States and who've helped make it a hit.

A very special thank you to the team who devoted countless hours and sleepless nights to this publication: Jennifer Buckley, Spiria Fearon, Amy Henderson, Leah Marie Fairbank, Diane Wood, Len Beech, Jennifer Smith, Lisa DiMona, Jenny Govier, Greg Ioannou, David Menzies, and the entire team at John Wiley & Sons. Your efforts and understanding of the vision have not gone unnoticed.

I'd like to express my gratitude to the amazing *Rich Bride Poor Bride* wedding planners and their hours of commitment to the show and this book. Your advice and expertise are the best in the world: Thank you.

A very special thank you goes out to the couples who have been featured on the show as well as those who have lent the images of their wedding day to this publication; you have been instrumental in making this resource guide a reality.

Thank you to Christopher Gentile and his photo studio for his cover shots. Your continued support and expertise throughout the making of this planning guide have been invaluable.

Thank you to our amazing photographers for your contributions; your photos have made *Your Ultimate Wedding Planning Guide* exactly that, and we couldn't have done it without you.

The following list includes the individuals who have committed their time, knowledge and support to the making of *Rich Bride Poor Bride*. We'd like to extend a very special thank you to the entire team at Buck Productions Inc.: Patricia Hollinger, Jim Kiriakakis, Stephen Hickey, Andrew Murray, Patricia Bush, Mark Peacock, Misty Tyson, Jennifer Couke, Jon Dobson, Joanna Puchala, Jonathan Garcia-Mainou, Toni Thomson, Christiane Galley, Crystal Mancini, Sarah Vingoe, Melanie Smith, Emily Pengelly, Doug Murray, Chris Veinot, Morgan Passi, Ann Pirvu, and all of the other amazing production crew members and talents who help make each episode of *Rich Bride Poor Bride* the success that it is.

Finally we'd like to thank the fans of the show. Without you this book would not be possible. This planning guide offers you the same valuable information, resources, ideas, and content you get from *Rich Bride Poor Bride*, so now you can put down the pen and paper and enjoy the show!

The red couch has become a bit of an icon. It's where newlyweds and seasoned veterans alike reflect on what they went through to get to "I do." Budgets may change over time, but the memories are always entertaining.

WE tv viewers watch *Rich Bride Poor Bride* not only for the inherent drama that planning a big wedding provides, but also for the tried-and-true tips the wedding planners offer. I love that the professional secrets are shared in one fun book, so any bride, with any budget, can be wedding savvy.

—Kim Martin
General Manager
WE tv

Offering an entertaining and hilarious look at the process behind planning a walk down the aisle, *Rich Bride Poor Bride* has been a hit on Slice since its launch—striking a chord with our viewers who appreciate all the commotion, meltdowns, and fabulous endings of a wedding. *Your Ultimate Wedding Planning Guide* is a brilliant accompaniment to the series and will be indispensable for couples as they plan their perfect day—without worrying about the price tag.

—Vanessa Case
Vice President, Content
Slice™

I Do.

But at WHAT COST?

Rich Bride Poor Bride

Christy & Tony

Re-live your favorite episodes: the ones that made you laugh, made you cry...and made you cringe.

Jennifer & Matt

Jennifer thought that once she had a vision for the wedding, the rest would just fall into place. Little did she know there was a ton of work to be done!

Any fan of **Rich Bride Poor Bride** knows that wedding planners are the heroes of the show. They're also the indispensable sources of the information in this book. As you'll soon discover, their candid advice and clever Top Ten Tips, garnered through years of experience, will guide you through every aspect of your wedding day.

Allister Reid

Allister Reid, along with his talented team at **Platinum Desk Concierge Service**, is responsible for lending style and flair to all sorts of events. With over 10 years' experience in event planning, he loves the challenge of planning a wedding on any budget. He can make a couple's dreams for their day come true, no matter what they want to spend. In addition to his planning talents, he is also an interior designer and personal shopper—handy skills to have for making sure every detail is looked after.

Allister has designed events for corporate clients like Ethan Allen, Louis Vuitton, and Bacardi, and has dealt with budgets as big as $750,000. His biggest challenge, however, was dealing with a bride who wanted a hotel to change the carpeting in its largest ballroom.

Angelique Sobschak

Angelique is the well-known president of **Angelique's Weddings and Events**, although she started out planning fundraisers and special business events as owner of Real Models and Talent Agency. Since 1994, she has coordinated weddings ranging from small gatherings for a few thousand dollars to large gala events with generous budgets.

Although Angelique's company also plans events other than weddings, her real passion is helping couples plan for their day. She'll do everything she can to make it special—she has even sourced a tiger for a magician's wedding.

Ann-Marie Daniel-Barker

As an experienced image consultant, Ann-Marie Daniel-Barker knows the importance of first impressions. She

brings the same sensibility to event planning, which she's been doing for 12 years with her company, **Prestige Image Consultants**. She can work anywhere, and with any budget, no matter how small. She's created intimate beach weddings in Jamaica, large-scale penthouse galas, and everything in between.

Ann-Marie is well-known for exceptional personal service, but even she has her limits. She was once asked to lend money to clients who had overspent their tiny budget—and she respectfully declined.

Chantel Walker and Charmaine Burke

Chantel Walker and Charmaine Burke tend to finish each other's sentences and answer each other's email. Strange habits for even the most dedicated business partners. But not only are they co-owners of **R&R Wedding and Event Designs**,

they are also sisters. After Charmaine, an experienced event planner, helped Chantel plan her wedding, they didn't want to stop. Soon Chantel's wedding guests were asking them to plan their weddings, and a business was born.

R&R stands for "rest and relax," which is exactly what Chantel and Charmaine have in mind for their clients. They aim to minimize a couple's stress and maximize their joy at every stage of the planning process, while creating unique events that reflect each couple's style.

David Connolly

David Connolly has 15 years of experience in planning an amazing array of events, from intimate weddings to high-profile fashion shows. His company, **theideashop**, has a global reputation for delivering outstanding production values and has an impressive celebrity client base that runs the gamut from Calvin Klein to RuPaul.

David approaches wedding planning with not just an eye to delivering on-time, on-budget weddings, but weddings that reflect the true personalities of the bride and groom. He believes that a wedding should make all the couple's dreams come true—even if those dreams involve him sourcing a rhinestone-encrusted wedding cake.

David Vallee

After the shortest professional career ever in the theater and a stint in politics, David Vallee opened a bistro called Fabulous Nobodies, and then added a catering department. He quickly fell in love with party planning, particularly weddings, and planned and catered his first legal gay wedding at his restaurant. After working for two prominent catering companies, he opened his own, **David Vallee Entertains**, in 2004.

Because of David's reputation and the company's ability to provide full-service event planning as well as catering, it has become one of the fastest growing planning and catering companies around. But even this multitalented guy has his challenges—including handling a bride who stabbed her mother with a fork.

Heidi Allen

Heidi Allen is the wedding guru. She's an award-winning wedding photographer, editor-in-chief of *Brides to Remember* magazine, and owner of a huge and gorgeous bridal salon.

So naturally, busy as she is, she has also parlayed her 15 years of experience in the industry into wedding planning with her company, **Weddings Heidi Style**.

Heidi's known for her warm, outspoken, no-nonsense approach to planning and negotiating. Her clients know they're in good hands when she's on the scene, and that she'll deal with any crisis—no matter how unlikely—quickly and professionally so that they don't have to.

Karina Lemke

Karina Lemke knows planning a wedding can be a time-consuming venture: The average couple spends over 200 hours planning their big day. So she makes it easy for her clients, guiding them through the process from start to finish and making sure they never make the wrong choice, whether it be over-the-top expenditures or jack-o'-lantern centerpieces.

Besides planning events, Karina owns **Posies Flower Shop**. The shop has a strong celebrity client base, with fans like Kate Hudson and Cher, and has garnered lots of media attention and accolades. However, Karina is still willing to do whatever it takes for any client, including sorting through 2,000 pieces of silverware to find matching forks.

Please turn to page 205 for our fabulous planners' contact information.

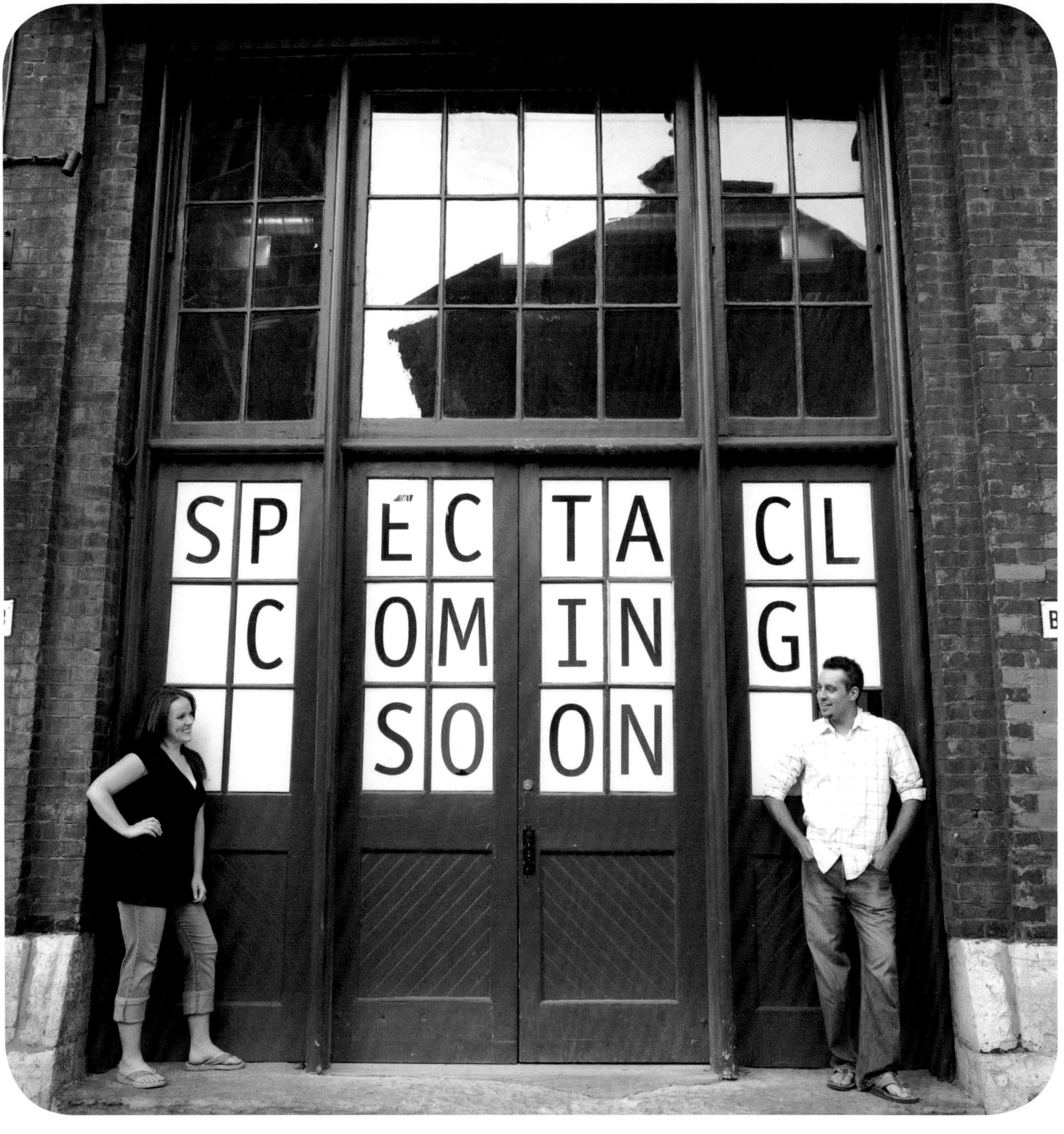
SPECTACL
COMING
SOON

In the BEGINNING

Hey, you guys are getting married! Congratulations, and welcome to one of the craziest, happiest roller coaster rides you'll ever be on. *Rich Bride Poor Bride* chronicles the dramas of dozens of anxious couples as they negotiate their way toward wedded bliss. As newlyweds, they return to sit on the red couch and share their journey with you. As you plan your own wedding, some of the most outrageous moments from the show will suddenly seem completely sensible. You'll understand their expressions of joy when all their dreams come true, and the fond memories and sage advice of the not-so-newlyweds who also share our red couch.

Your experiences over the next several months will challenge and stimulate you, will be filled with opportunities for learning, and will present you with limitless ideas for creating your own dream come true. You will discover how much your family and friends care about you as they gladly volunteer to help you with seemingly impossible tasks. And your relationship with each other will become stronger and deeper as you work together to achieve the ideal celebration of your love: an unforgettable, kick-ass party.

This all sounds wonderful, but where do you start? As you gazed into each other's eyes after that fateful proposal, no doubt a myriad of questions already started to pop into your heads. What happens next? When can I tell everyone I know? How are we ever going to pay for this?!?! Don't worry. Eight experienced wedding planners are on your side. You've seen them in action on *Rich Bride Poor Bride*, skillfully negotiating with vendors, soothing frazzled nerves, and making the impossible happen. Now they're working for you. Throughout this book, you'll find their indispensable tips for navigating through thousands of options, maximizing any budget, and doing it all with minimal stress.

Faye & Leon
married: 44 years
wedding budget:
$2,000

It was love at first sight for me.

They always say it has to be love at first sight for at least one of the parties involved, right? Well in this case it was, which is nice to know.

⚙ The Dynamic Duo

One of the most important things to remember is that the two of you are in this together. Take advantage of each other's support, and work as a team to make your dream wedding happen. Planning your wedding is an opportunity to learn and grow together, and a chance to take on anything that's thrown at you as a united front, as two against the world. Of course, you're not really fighting a battle; sometimes it just feels a bit like it when you're hounded by dissenting opinions and stubborn service providers. Just knowing that you have one person who's firmly on your side, not to mention a huge network of supportive people who only want the best for you, will make you eager for any challenge. Bring on the broken-down limo, the snowstorm in June, the hidden corkage fees your venue charges at the last moment! Nothing can stop you from getting married.

☀ Let's Make It a Date

Once you've put a notice in the paper or sent a mass email announcing your engagement to everyone you know (including anyone who might casually pass it on to your exes), there are a few key issues to get out of the way before you rush off to the dress shop. Everything you plan will depend on three things: the date, the budget, and the theme. The next couple of chapters will help you determine your budget and your theme, or vision, for your wedding day. First, talk with each other about the kind of wedding you want to have, and

A great marriage is the result of exceptional teamwork. Strangely enough, so is a great wedding.

when that wedding could happen. If you imagine a small ceremony on a beach, is it a local beach in July or a tropical beach in November? Or do you imagine fall colors or a wintery chalet? Or a garden full of flowers and a couple hundred guests having cocktails on the lawn? While running through the possibilities, keep in mind that your wedding date can significantly affect your budget.

Planning a wedding for the most popular weekends means booking some vendors over a year in advance, and sometimes two years. It also means that these vendors can charge as much as they like. If you're determined to be married on a Saturday in July,

> **ANGELIQUE ON TAKING A BREAK:** *Take breaks from wedding planning to rekindle the romance and remind yourselves why you're getting married in the first place. Do things together that make you think of each other: a walk by the ocean or a hike up a mountain; a lazy Sunday brunch or a trip to the go-kart track.*

"When's the Big Day?"
The questions begin right after the engagement. If sun isn't crucial to your wedded bliss, consider an off-season date for more budgetary freedom.

your wedding will probably be sunny and beautiful, but you may not get your preferred venue, photographer, and DJ, or you may have to pay through the nose to get them. If time of year or day of the week are irrelevant to you, you can free up room in your budget before you even open your first spreadsheet. **Because vendors are eager for your business in their downtime, they're more likely to charge favorable rates if you book on days other than Saturday or in the off-season.** Granted, a Wednesday wedding might not be the most practical or romantic one you can imagine, but a cocktail party on a Friday evening or an afternoon luncheon on Sunday can be. And you don't have to have

your pictures taken in a summer garden for them to be remarkable. Since the photo shoot is really the only significant amount of time you spend outdoors in many weddings, it's just as easy to get married in the autumn or winter. Rich fall colors, or a cosy fire and frosted windows, will make your photos stunning and your guests feel relaxed and toasty warm.

Contrary to what you might think, fewer attendants often means less stress and more support.

Edith & Kam
A pricey ring was almost a deal-breaker for Kam. Lucky for Edith (but not the caterer), he caved.

Begin by having a few dates in mind. When you start looking at venues, you'll need to be flexible because they'll likely have already booked some dates. If you're having the ceremony and reception at separate locations, don't put any deposits down until you know you can get both for the same date. Okay, that may sound obvious, but in the excitement of closing your first deal, you'll probably just want to get it done. Finally, you'll have an answer when people pester you for a date! And the rest will all work itself out, right? Maybe, but why rush? Treat your platinum card like gold, and don't waste deposits on things you're not sure of. You'll need that money later for really important things like shoes and limos. Of course, if you absolutely must have your reception in a certain venue but could care less where your ceremony is, book the venue if you can get it. However, you may find that venues are eager to book for less popular dates. **If you're flexible with dates, use it to your advantage and negotiate reduced rates or added services as a condition of renting a venue.**

⚙ Circle of Friends

When you start planning, you'll think a lot about the resources you have available: friends with connections; willing sources of cheap labor; people you can escape with when you need a drink or a trip to the movies. Hey wait, that sounds a lot like a wedding party!

Many brides have picked their attendants well in advance of their engagement. And equally as many brides—and probably most grooms—haven't given it a second thought. Chantel and Charmaine suggest you think seriously about who you want in your party, and especially about how many you want, before you ask anyone. Pick people that you can rely on and that you want to spend time with, like your brothers and sisters (okay, maybe not!), your golfing buddies, and the girlfriends you hit the martini bars with once a month. And pick just a few attendants. You may feel so close to your entire softball

> **CHANTEL AND CHARMAINE ON YOUR EXPANDING ENTOURAGE:**
> *Keep your wedding party small—under ten in total. The size of the wedding party really affects expenses at all levels: more flowers, transportation, gifts, and food for the rehearsal dinner, not to mention more chaos on the wedding day.*

team that you want them all to be your attendants, but that enthusiasm could fizzle when they start arguing over what dress to wear. There are plenty of other jobs to be filled for those you'd love to include in your day but who may not rank higher than your three brothers and your best friend since kindergarten. You'll need people to give readings, light candles, hand out programs, act as emcee, and tell people where they're seated at the reception, for instance. Hold some friends in reserve for these important tasks.

Bridesmaids are expected to help plan your shower and the all-important bachelorette party. They can also help you with menial tasks such as sealing envelopes, and they should do everything they can to make your wedding day go smoothly. The maid or matron of honor will lead the charge, and can accompany you to appointments and act as another sounding board for your outrageous ideas. Groomsmen, on the other hand, aren't expected to do much: plan the bachelor party, usher guests at the ceremony, and make sure the groom gets to the wedding. The best man might also hold onto the wedding rings and any checks that need to be given to vendors at the wedding. But that's not all these amazing friends can do for you. Remember

that not only have they agreed to stand by you, they've agreed to help. If you're just too swamped to do something yourself, you've got a bunch of people at your disposal. At least one of them should be able to pick up the favors. They'll all be more than willing to help you choose wine.

Your wedding party members are now your personal slaves! So make use of their talents and goodwill, and learn to delegate.

☼ It's "I Do," not "What Are We Going to Do?"

Feeling a bit overwhelmed? Don't worry about it! Organization is the key to being the bride and groom who keep their cool. Our planners offer their Top Ten Tips for avoiding planning chaos on page 21, but one of the most important tools you can use is right here. The following checklist tells you what you need to do and when you need to do it. And this book will show you how.

A List to Get You Started

One Year Earlier or More

- [ ] Decide on the kind of wedding you want: small or large, formal or casual
- [ ] Figure out your budget
- [ ] Pick some potential dates
- [ ] Reserve ceremony and reception venues
- [ ] Pick your wedding party
- [ ] Start your guest list
- [ ] Register for a few things in case people want to buy you engagement gifts
- [ ] Drop hints to your parents that you'd like an engagement party

Nine Months to One Year

- [ ] Hire a wedding planner
- [ ] Visit a florist to see what's in season
- [ ] Book an officiant and have your first meeting with him or her
- [ ] Order the wedding dress
- [ ] Book your photographer
- [ ] Book your florist
- [ ] Register for gifts
- [ ] Plan your honeymoon
- [ ] Start tasting wine

Six to Nine Months

- [ ] Book your entertainment (DJ, band, ceremony musicians, etc.)
- [ ] Order stationery
- [ ] Order bridesmaids' dresses
- [ ] Choose your wedding bands
- [ ] Reserve limousines
- [ ] Order or begin assembling favors
- [ ] Order your wedding cake
- [ ] Book rooms at a hotel close to the reception venue for out-of-town guests
- [ ] Look into marriage license requirements

Three to Six Months

- [ ] Finalize the guest list
- [ ] Send save the date cards or contact out-of-town guests
- [ ] Book your caterer
- [ ] Choose rental items, such as linens and china
- [ ] Reserve rental items, if not provided by your venue or caterer
- [ ] Finalize your menu
- [ ] Have engagement photos taken
- [ ] Enroll in a marriage course
- [ ] Order tuxes or buy suits for groom and groomsmen
- [ ] Book hair and makeup stylists and make appointments for consultations
- [ ] Choose the readers, speakers, and emcee

Two Months

- ☐ Mail the invitations
- ☐ Make appointments for dress fittings
- ☐ Meet with your officiant to finalize ceremony details and book rehearsal
- ☐ Have the programs printed
- ☐ Buy gifts for your wedding party
- ☐ Buy gifts for each other
- ☐ Make spa and nail appointments, and book a massage therapist for the wedding day
- ☐ Decide on your wedding vows or start writing your own
- ☐ Schedule the final dress fitting

One Month

- ☐ Have hair and makeup consultations
- ☐ Apply for your marriage license
- ☐ Buy liquor, if you're providing your own
- ☐ Plan the rehearsal dinner

Two Weeks

- ☐ Confirm details with all of your vendors
- ☐ Get hair cut and/or colored
- ☐ Get a facial
- ☐ Write your thank you speech
- ☐ Make sure bridesmaids have their dresses
- ☐ Call guests who haven't replied
- ☐ Deliver song lists to DJ or band
- ☐ Confirm honeymoon and wedding night reservations
- ☐ Arrange seating plan
- ☐ Buy any missing small items (guestbook, unity candle, etc.)
- ☐ Create seating chart and place cards
- ☐ Give itineraries to wedding party members and parents
- ☐ Give itineraries to vendors (caterer, photographer, emcee, DJ or band, etc.)
- ☐ Go on a date (with each other, that is) and don't talk about the wedding

One Week

- ☐ Pack for the honeymoon
- ☐ Give final numbers to caterer, venue, and rental company
- ☐ Confirm delivery details for flowers and cake
- ☐ Ask someone to return rentals after the wedding
- ☐ Write any checks you'll need for final payments on the wedding day
- ☐ Make sure there's enough money in the bank account to cover those checks while you're away
- ☐ Pick up the tuxedos
- ☐ Pick up the wedding dress
- ☐ Get manicure and pedicure
- ☐ Deliver favors and décor items to reception venue
- ☐ Have the rehearsal and the rehearsal dinner
- ☐ Give your wedding party their gifts
- ☐ Give your marriage license to your officiant
- ☐ Review checklist and itinerary

To pull off a fairytale wedding, you'll need to rely on the mundane: to-do lists, schedules, file folders, and other romantic accoutrements.

Okay, don't panic about the giant list. Sure, you've got *so* much to do, but this is your key to sliding through the process in style. Plus, you've got an army of people willing to help you for free, and someone to lean on when it all gets a bit much. Not to mention that at the end of it, when you've checked everything off, you'll be married! You'll be jetting off on your honeymoon, opening gifts, moving into a new home, starting a family, growing old together…

Words of Wisdom for the Planning Process

*The **Rich Bride Poor Bride** wedding planners have been through this whole crazy drill many, many times. Trust their experience and advice for starting your planning off right.*

1 Dream big: "Blue Sky" your wedding dreams first as though there is absolutely no budget. If money was not an issue, what would you do? That will give you a wonderful base of inspiration that can ultimately be distilled into affordable reality. You will be surprised how many elements of your dream can be realized on the day.

2 While the bride and groom are the stars of the wedding day, they are not the only participants. Try to be respectful of the reasonable wishes of family and friends—especially if they are helping you financially. **Stick to your wishes on important points but concede** on some of the details that will make mothers, fathers, and others feel included.

3 Listen to your heart. The day should reflect your instincts, your desires, and your dreams coming true. You will be bombarded by input; some of it will be valuable, some won't. And while you're listening— listen to each other. **Both the bride and the groom should have equal say.**

4 **Do not try to satisfy everyone.** A wedding affects many family members, all of whom will have their own ideas. Be sure to listen and remember that compromise can be your best friend.

5 **It's your day to shine, so don't be afraid to personalize your affair.** Traditions are traditions for a reason and should be considered, but there are wonderful ways to put a personal spin on an old-school idea that makes your day less cookie-cutter. Play the wedding march, but if it suits you, have it played by a rock band, or a marching band.

6 Think outside the box. If you don't like wedding cake, you don't have to serve it. **Let them eat cake at someone else's wedding.**

7 **Always make sure your food and dress are spectacular.** The two things people always talk about after a wedding are the bride's dress and the food.

8 Wedding planning can cause a great deal of stress. **Be aware of each** other's stress thresholds. If you notice that one of you is nearing that threshold, take a short break from your wedding planning and do something fun together.

9 Do not forget about romance. It's the reason you're getting married. **Take time away from wedding planning to be with each other.** A romantic dinner, a bike ride—whatever you both like to do together. Just don't discuss the wedding plans!

10 **If it all seems too much, elope and have a big party when you return.** That way you have no stress and still get the gifts!

Get Down with YOUR BUDGET

A wedding can be a quickie ceremony at city hall followed by an intimate family dinner.

A wedding can be a week-long vacation on a tropical island. And a wedding can be a blow-out

ceremony and reception complete with limos, formal dinner, and rock band. The determining

factors? Your personal style—or your level of tolerance for planning—and your budget.

After all, it's "I Do," but at what cost? One of the most stressful elements in wedding

planning is deciding how to spend your money, and the last thing you want is to enter your

marriage in debt. The average wedding runs about $200 to $250 per guest. That means an average 100-person wedding will cost around $20,000 to $25,000, and will balloon to $60,000 to $75,000 for an average 300-person event. Take note of the word "average": A big-city wedding in a five-star hotel is not average. Neither is a small-town wedding in a community hall. So with that in mind, determine what kind of wedding you would like and what amount of money you have available.

✿ Picking Up the Tab

Western tradition says that the groom's parents pay for the wedding rings, the groom's outfit, the marriage license, the rehearsal dinner, personal flowers for their family, and the bar at the reception, and the bride's family pays for everything else. Few follow that formula anymore, and many parents just give couples a lump sum to do with as they please. Or so they say. But there's no such thing as a free six-course dinner for 200. They may promise that they won't get involved and you can have the wedding you want, but at some point they'll add their two cents and expect you to listen. Angelique has seen many couples deal with meddling families, including parents who inflate the guest list even if they're not paying. As a result, more and more couples are paying for their weddings on their own so that they don't have to listen to anyone else if they don't want to. Regardless of who's paying, set the rules right from the beginning—tell your parents how much input you're willing to accept, keeping in mind how much they are contributing. But remember that one of the reasons they want to be involved is because they care, so even if the two of you are paying for everything, be willing to listen occasionally. Your dad might be on the right track when he suggests you stash the beer in a canoe full of ice.

Your perfect wedding can happen on any budget. You've just got to be creative and willing to compromise on the things that don't matter so much. And hey, that ballroom probably wasn't really your style anyway.

❀ Reality Check

Once you know how much money you have to work with, make a realistic budget. If you want to copy the latest Hollywood wedding you saw in a magazine, first check with your agent to make sure that seven-figure movie deal is secure. Wedding costs tend to spiral out of control as couples or their families try to outdo the last wedding that took place in their circle of friends and family. Keep costs in check from Day One. Create a specific line-item budget, allocating dollar amounts to different areas of the wedding, and stick to it. As you can see in almost every episode of *Rich Bride Poor Bride*, couples love to go a little over budget on "just this one thing." Which ends up being everything.

The biggest influence on your budget is the number of guests. Start with a dollar amount that you can afford, and use Angelique's exercise to check if it's realistic:

1. Multiply the number of guests you want by $90 for food and bar.

2. The formality of your wedding will influence the cost of everything else. Multiply your guest numbers by $150 for a casual wedding, $200 for semiformal, and $250 for formal.

3. Add the two numbers together, plus taxes and gratuities, to see what your wedding could cost.

Now that you've got your number, it's time to build a spreadsheet. This will be your guiding force for the next several months, but that doesn't mean it has to be painful. Grab a glass of wine—just don't spill it on the keyboard, or you'll be adding that to your budget. Plug the percentages that follow into the spreadsheet to see how much you can spend in each area.

You may think you're ready to get married, but is your wallet? This is gonna cost you!

Adjust them to fit your priorities, but no creative accounting. If you blow the bank on the invitations, you might want to consider downgrading your limo bus to a minivan.

Ceremony: 4%–8%
Location fee, officiant's fee, janitor's fee

Reception: 40%–60%
Rentals, food, bar, cake, cutting fee, favors, décor, tips

Attire: 7%–15%
Bride's gown, alterations, accessories, hair, and makeup: 5%–10%
Groom's suit or tuxedo, shoes: 2%–5%

Wedding Rings: 2%–5%
Rings, engraving

Flowers: 9%–12%
Personal, ceremonial, and reception

Music: 4%–10%
Ceremony and reception

Photo/Video: 8%–15%
Photographer, engagement photos, prints, albums, videographer

Attendants' Gifts: 2%–5%

Transportation: 2%–6%
Limo, guest shuttle, parking

Stationery: 4%–5%
Announcements, save the date cards, invitations, postage, programs, guestbook and pen, thank you notes

Miscellaneous: 9%–20%
Wedding license, wedding planner, event insurance, legal fees, gown preservation, bouquet preservation, wedding night hotel room

Add 10% for unexpected expenses, because they will come up. The reception takes up the lion's share of the budget, as it involves catering, bar, décor, and rentals, which may just be linen and china but could also include a tent, tables and chairs, and porta-potties if your wedding is outdoors. When you are budgeting for the number of guests, you can usually count on approximately 20% of your guest list not attending, says Angelique.

❄ Ice Sculptures, Palm Readers, and Other Essentials

Strangely enough, the amount of money spent doesn't actually equal the amount of happiness on the wedding day. In fact, if you find yourself opening gifts during the wedding so you can pay the caterer, it'll likely be quite the opposite. If you're drooling over champagne fountains and strolling magicians, it's time to prioritize. Try not to get caught up in "we have to have this." You will spend yourself to death—maybe literally. Angelique once had to source a full-grown tiger for a wedding. The going rate was $1,250—before insurance, which was deemed necessary in case the tiger decided to assert its rightful place in the food chain. The tiger? Not so necessary. And the list of extravagant and unnecessary frills goes on and on, from $1,000 for a chocolate fountain, to $1,500 for fireworks, to $10,000 for a custom-made music video. In the case of weddings, *do* sweat the small stuff. It becomes big stuff awfully quickly when you multiply it by 300 guests.

Time to get your priorities in order. Love good food and music, but not so hung up on designer duds? Adjust your budget accordingly.

Prioritize by focusing on the things that matter to the two of you, and find creative alternatives for everything else. The *Rich Bride Poor Bride* wedding planners have endless suggestions on ways to cut costs. For instance, never order enough wedding cake to feed everyone. Most people don't eat the cake—they're usually still stuffed from dinner—so order enough for half the number of guests or just a touch more. Another tip is to brace yourself for the hard sell.

The wedding industry is built on up-selling, but don't fall prey. Be firm with vendors and with yourself. **Cap the guest list: Weddings are more expensive by the dozen, so invite only people you actually know.** And as you'll find throughout this book, some important parts of your wedding, like invitations and the wedding dress, don't have to be expensive to be perfect.

❀ Getting Your Priorities Straight

There are some things guests always remember about weddings, and they're usually the things that personally affect them: food, music, and booze. The food has to be exceptional: It should look appetizing, it has to be the right temperature, and your guests shouldn't have to wait too long for it. If you can afford a band, get one, but make sure you see it perform first so you know if the musicians are versatile, able to take requests, and used to playing weddings. And do everything you can to avoid having a cash bar. If you can't afford a host bar, you're inviting too many people.

Of course, if it's common practice where you live to invite the whole town after dinner and charge a minimal amount for drinks, and you decide to do the same, you may feel like a show-off—or a little nervous—without a cash bar. Do what you feel is appropriate, but if at all possible, buy your guests some drinks. Another indisputable priority is photography. You'll be stuck with your wedding pictures forever, so you'll want to make sure they won't make your children roll their eyes at you years from now.

Rose & John
married: 20 years
wedding budget: $7,500

John just kept on signing those checks, and I guess after 20 years of marriage nothing has really changed.

Yeah, she's right!

❀ Your Wedding Superhero

An optional expense that will likely save you money in the end is a wedding planner. (Prepare for shameless self-promotion!) Wedding planning is a full-time job, and you probably already have one of those. You can't spare the kind of time needed to research the best options, find deals and low-cost alternatives, and negotiate to get the best value. Planners do this every day.

Tina & Fabio
Time for a much needed budget review. Is Tina in denial, and is Fabio in the dark?

They charge either a flat rate (starting at $1,000) or a percentage of the wedding's overall budget (usually 10% to 20%). They will help you with the entire process, or you

> **ANGELIQUE ON GETTING AWAY FROM IT ALL:** *When couples are working with a very tight budget, the first thing I say is, "Why don't you have a destination wedding?" They're less expensive than traditional weddings. You'll get a group discount, and you can still have a casual party. You can have a beautiful wedding on an even tinier budget if it's just the two of you, and you get a great vacation!*

can just hire them for the day of the wedding to make sure everything goes off without a hitch. Wedding planners will work with any budget, and will also keep you on track with that budget, acting as your voice of reason when you're dangerously

close to going over. A few tips for making it easier for your planner to plan: Pay up front so she won't have to take out a second mortgage to book your DJ. Take planners' suggestions to heart. They've been through this many times before. Don't expect them to work miracles, but if you treat them with respect they'll be able—and more than willing—to do everything possible to make your dream day come true.

Ann-Marie has lots of tales of clients who have expected services that just weren't in the contract. Take a close look at the contract and you won't find any of the following: three a.m. calls to discuss

You make the perfect pair, but a third person might help you pull off the perfect wedding.

barely formed ideas for centerpieces, money-lending services when you go over budget against your planner's advice, or the dress off her back when yours becomes ripped beyond repair. Ann-Marie even had parents ask her to disinvite guests that they had invited behind their children's backs! (A good reason to limit access to your planner's phone number.)

❀ License to Spend

Spending more money won't make you any more married. Unless you forget to shell out for the marriage license—that

can definitely affect how married you are. You're likely to forget your budget as you get caught up in the process of planning and as you're bombarded with tons of exciting ideas at bridal shows and wedding websites. So come back to your budget on a regular basis to make sure you're on track. And remember that less is often more. If you do a few things well, rather than try chaotically to do everything, you'll create a much better impression and, as a bonus, stay sane — and solvent.

Unless the sky's the limit, sticking to a budget is hard.
But starting a marriage in debt is a lot harder.

Rich Bride Poor Bride loves wedding planners, and you should too. They wear many hats and draw on many skills in order to make your dreams come true.

1 **Wedding planners are first and foremost consultants on everything weddings.** They will work with you to fulfill your vision for the day, and they'll come up with creative solutions to make it happen on budget.

2 **They act as your representative in the scary world of vendors.** They know vendors in a way you can't: not only their reputations for quality or timeliness, but if there's any bad blood between vendors you're interested in. They will negotiate with vendors on your behalf in order to get the best possible value, which may not necessarily be the lowest price. Often vendors are more willing to throw in extras for the same price rather than lower their price.

3 They are supreme organizers. **A wedding planner will prepare an itinerary for you**, and will keep you on track. Planners know when things need to be done, so they'll never let you fall behind.

4 **Many planners specialize in destination weddings or cultural weddings, so they are able to help you with whatever wedding you envision.**

5 **Wedding planners have financial skills to keep you on budget.** So when they call that meeting about how you're about to go drastically and irrevocably over budget, listen to them.

6 Many wedding planners say they find themselves acting as therapists from time to time. **When the pressure of competing interests or difficult decisions builds up, they become a shoulder to cry on.**

7 **Often, they're marriage counselors too.** They've seen enough weddings to know the emotions and arguments involved. They will help you to put these in perspective and see the real focus of the wedding: each other.

8 On the day of the wedding, **wedding planners are your on-site ringmaster and problem-solver**, making sure everything runs smoothly, and if it doesn't, that you don't have to deal with it.

9 **They're discreet.** Don't worry, your mother will never know what you said about her in a fit of rage.

10 However, few will act as your taxi service, courier service, bouncer, or bank. They aren't available all hours of the day, they can't accompany you to every appointment—and they can't meet you on Saturdays. **They're usually busy on Saturday.**

Va-va-voom YOUR VENUE

Your party will suck up the biggest part of your budget, and it should. What do you remember from other weddings? Likely you were really only there for the party, if you're honest with yourself, so make it a priority in your budget. If your budget is tiny, don't worry about being limited to a potluck dinner and a BYOB bar. You have a huge range of options at any price, and one of the most versatile options is your venue. But before you look for the perfect party place, think about your party style. Whether your style is urban chic, back-to-nature, or anything else under the sun, your reception is your chance to throw the party of your dreams.

🌸 Setting the Scene

When David Connolly meets with a bride and groom, they either know exactly what they want or they have absolutely no idea. In the latter case, he tries to determine their personal styles and use that to guide the style of the wedding. If the bride has picked her dress already, that tells him everything he needs to know: A simple, straight gown belongs in a completely different wedding than a crinoline princess gown. Another guideline is how you want your guests to feel. Should they be excited and energized, or pampered and relaxed, or do you want them to feel like they're falling in love again? Use that intention to help guide your decisions. You need to start somewhere—whether it be with colors, textures, or just a feeling—because the choices are limitless. But never lose sight of the real purpose of the day, reminds Ann-Marie. Make choices that reflect both of you, and try to make both your dreams come true in some aspect of the wedding. Besides marrying the partner of your dreams, of course.

Julie & Derick

Derick dreamt of a wintery wedding—in a campus bar. When his spending snowballed, Heidi and Julie had to rein him in.

Your wedding could also be about your heritage. Making your culture a significant and consistent part of your wedding is an easy way to choose food, décor, and entertainment. If many of your guests are from a different culture, they'll appreciate the opportunity to experience something exotic. It will also give them something to talk about. One wedding David planned started out with a square dance before dinner.

The bride and groom chose to do this to recognize their western upbringing. When they entered the room, the bride lifted her dress to reveal cowboy boots. All the guests were asked to participate in the dance, which sounds potentially disastrous, but because everyone felt ridiculous together, they connected with one another and had a great time. It was a successful icebreaker, and the energy carried on throughout the evening.

Start with something simple—a color, an object, or even the dress—and build your theme around it.

Amy & Jay

An exotic setting is closer than you think. Between the group discounts, affordable wedding packages, and small guest lists, all-inclusive resorts are among the most budget-friendly venues going.

◉ X-treme Weddings

The theme of your wedding should be "we are in love," but if for you that means being in love in a winter wonderland or under the sea, David advises you to double your budget at the very least. A masked ball–themed wedding he once planned required a budget of $300,000. If you pick a theme, rather than just a style, you have to carry it throughout everything, from the invitations, to the clothing, to the food, to the entertainment. Another thing to keep in mind when considering a theme wedding, says Ann-Marie, is the comfort level of your guests. She once planned a pink wedding in which the bride

> **ANN-MARIE ON DOING THE IMPOSSIBLE:** *A couple wanted a winter wonderland wedding. With one catch: It was in Jamaica. I called all my contacts, found a snow-making machine, and had it shipped by boat. I wasn't sure we could pull it off, but it did look like a winter wonderland. Many guests had never seen snow, so they loved it.*

insisted on Barbie dolls as centerpieces, and many of the guests found the décor creepy. Angelique planned an S&M-themed wedding for a goth couple, which definitely had the potential to be creepy, but the guest list had been carefully considered.

◉ One-Stop Shopping

You've probably been to the same banquet halls time and again for weddings. They're your full-service option for venues, offering catering, food, booze, plenty of parking, and maybe a gazebo for pictures or the ceremony. Seems like the perfect answer, right?

It can be if you're happy with a cookie-cutter wedding. Not that there's anything wrong with that, but you'll be limited in what you can do with décor, what kind of food you have, and what kind of wine you serve. You will also probably be competing with several other weddings if your venue is big enough. In one episode of *Rich Bride Poor Bride*, Angelique found that the venue had put up signs directing guests to the two receptions being held, but had spelled the bride's name wrong and had actually switched the names so that the groom was listed with a different bride! A lot of these venues can make it seem like your wedding was staged by a soap opera, says David Vallee. Besides the drama of ending up with the wrong bride or groom, that is.

❧ Been There, Done That

A banquet hall is cheap and easy, but your guests have seen it all before. Another easy option, with a bit more flair, is a hotel. **In fact, a hotel ballroom is the least expensive fine-food venue.** You're still limited on catering and wine, but the quality is usually a bit better, the location more convenient, and the price more reasonable. Plus, hotels often offer room discounts for you and your guests. You can usually get a package that includes service, dishes, bar, and food for between $100 and $150 per person. You'd have a hard time doing a gourmet sit-down dinner anywhere else for that price.

David suggests you look for a non-traditional venue to make your wedding memorable. Guests appreciate a unique venue, and they'll talk about it after your wedding. That's the kind of buzz you want. Look around your community for beautiful and unexpected locations, such as historic buildings and museums, and you'll be surprised at what unique spaces are available for rental. David has planned weddings

in breweries, cafés, farmers' markets, and vacant floors of office towers, to name a few. (For a list of more venue ideas, see Novel Venues for Uncommon Couples, page 175.) Even venues like barns and cellars can be transformed into formal settings. But be sure to let the space speak to you. Work with it, and don't try to create Versailles unless you're in a chateau. It's a lot less expensive to decorate if you're accenting what's there, not covering stuff up.

If your ideal venue is being renovated, don't rely on it being done when they say, or for it to look at all like you expected. There are always delays and changes in renovations, so don't rent sight unseen.

When choosing décor, work with what you've got. Keep the venue in mind for best effect and best bang for your buck.

Spectacular Settings

No need to book the nearest banquet hall.
Whether a castle or a barn or any place in between,
a unique venue makes for a fairytale wedding
and an adventure for your guests.

❂ Everything Including the Kitchen Sink

A reasonable rate is $20–$25 per person for a non-traditional venue. That doesn't include everything you'll have to bring in, which is, in fact, everything. But that's okay. It means you get your choice of caterer, wine, linen, china, and furniture, rather than being stuck with whatever the banquet hall or hotel provides. It also means that

> **CHANTEL AND CHARMAINE ON NOVEL HEAD TABLES:** *You can do so much with the head table when you have a small wedding party. To feel more involved in the party, opt for a long empire table in the middle of the room, with the wedding party seated on both sides, or a sweetheart table for just the bride and groom.*

potentially you have more control over your budget. However, expenses tend to soar when your options are limitless, so if you do use a non-traditional venue, keep a close watch on your budget.

When considering non-traditional venues, make sure there's running water and an area where a kitchen can be set up, if one isn't available. Consult with your caterer to see what facilities he'll need or how he can adapt the menu to work with what's there. Also make sure there are enough toilets. Lining up for toilets is right up there on the "what people talk about" list.

One place you can save money while improving quality is the bar. Keep it simple and limit the bar to wine, beer, a signature cocktail, and nonalcoholic options. Hire a couple of bartenders and buy your own liquor. You can usually return any unopened bottles, so don't be afraid to be generous. In the end, you'll spend money bringing things into a non-traditional venue, but you'll save money on liquor and improve the quality of every element of your wedding.

🏵 Under the Stars

Contrary to what you might think, weddings at home aren't necessarily cheap. They can be, if you have an intimate party for a couple dozen people in your backyard, but as the guest list grows, the expenses can get out of control. On top of catering, rentals, and all the standard expenses—which may have to be imported from a city if the local offerings aren't up to your standards—you'll also need a tent. Wishful thinking ain't going to keep the rain and cold away, so don't even think of trying to go without. Tents can cost around $1,200 to $1,500 for a small wedding, but there are endless options that can add to the cost, like a dance floor, windows, lights, and side tents for the caterers and porta-potties.

If you invite 300 guests, shell out for air conditioning, and get a floor for the whole tent, before you know it you'll have a small construction project on your hands.

Back to the porta-potties: the price you pay to get married in a meadow. **You'll need at least one washroom for every 50 guests; but you can get away with one or two less and save a bit of money by not worrying about gender-specific washrooms. Men don't need** them so much, so give the women more options. Which brings up another point: If you're getting married out-

**Lynne &
Lawrence**
married: 32 years
wedding budget:
$5,000

There were a few people we couldn't seat together, and it did make for problems.

But it was a good thing, because that was the side of the wedding planning that I gave to my mother.

An outdoor wedding is a magical setting. Picture the radiance of the setting sun, the warm, inviting glow of the tent, the twinkle of fairy lights in trees—wait, is that the best man behind that tree?

doors, get over your squeamishness about guys peeing against a tree in your backyard. It's a sign of a great party, if nothing else. And don't forget hand-washing stations. The catering staff will need to wash their hands, of course, and hopefully so will those guys in the backyard.

If you are getting married in a meadow rather than your yard, check with your township to see if you need a permit. You can do almost anything you want in your home, which includes your yard, but that may not apply to agricultural property. You'll also need to think about noise: If you haven't invited your neighbors, at least warn them.

The more candles, the merrier. Think in groupings and odd numbers, and include candles in unexpected places to make every corner of your party glow.

And transportation: Do you have enough room at your cottage for parking? Is there taxi service between the hotel you've reserved and your farm? Think about options for preventing drinking and driving, such as a bus or valet service. A good host wouldn't leave guests to figure out parking on their own. And if you don't take measures to offer alternate transportation, your party will come to an early end when half of your guests are designated drivers. These are all things that will bump up the expenses.

Having your wedding at home can be magical, though. Just the idea of getting married in the yard you used to play in, under the tree you used to climb, might be enough inspiration if you've got the space, the energy, and the budget. Imagine your mom helping the caterers in the kitchen, and your dad having an excuse to finish all those fix-it projects he's been stalling on. Then imagine leaving one last mess for them to clean up—with loads of help, of course—as you jet off on your honeymoon!

Getting to the big day requires organizational skills and stress-busting tactics. The following ideas will provide you with both:

1 As you plan, you will accumulate brochures, business cards, estimates, contracts, receipts, and clippings. **You'll need tools, all of which are easily accessible and inexpensive**: a large wall calendar or a computer program you can enter detailed information in, a journal for to-do lists, a three-ring binder with dividers and pouches for collecting ideas, and an accordion file for receipts and contracts.

2 Avoid feeling overwhelmed by the number of tasks ahead of you. **Stay organized by creating a to-do list**, the essential tool for tracking your progress and keeping your plans in order.

3 **Choose only one or two days a week to focus on your wedding preparations, and plan together.** This eliminates confusion as to who is planning what, and it also prevents the wedding planning from consuming your lives.

4 Weddings are not do-it-yourself projects. **If you want to do things yourself, choose things that can be done well in advance.** Guest gifts and personalized invitations can be done well ahead of time so you're not sent into a tailspin at the last moment.

5 **Dare to stay on schedule.** Schedules are like budgets: a pain to create, but your only chance at being able to enjoy your day. There should be many schedules: long-range, short-range, day-of, and one for every member of your party, with roles and responsibilities clearly outlined.

6 Your guest list will surely give you headaches, but be strong. **Once you have decided on the number of guests you would like to invite, stick to it.** Don't allow others to influence your decision.

7 **Know how to cut your guest list.** The first step is to go through the list and put an "A" or a "B" next to each name. The As are the absolute must-invites. The next step: Cut the B-list. Ask yourself these three questions: *Have I seen this person in the last 12 months?*

Have I talked to him in the last six months? Did I send her a Christmas card last year? If you answer "No" to any of the above, feel free to cut away.

8 **The two of you should plan the seating chart alone.** Don't let anyone else help. Fights often occur when family members get involved, so cut down on the number of opinions.

9 **Expect the best, but prepare for the worst.** Know a company that can deliver a plastic cake if yours collapses; have something to wear if red wine is spilled on your gown; and know whom to call if your step-mom passes out from too much champagne.

10 **If you don't have the time or resources, hiring a wedding planner will help ease your stress.** He or she will negotiate contracts, recommend reliable vendors, and keep you on time and on budget.

All Things PAPER

You could spend half your planning time just sorting through stationery options. Save-the-dates, maps, programs, place cards, menu cards, monogrammed napkins, tags for favors... the choices are a little overwhelming. But the one thing that is absolutely necessary, in one form or another, is the invitation. Your invitation is the first chance to show people what your wedding's all about. So you should go all out on the 100% cotton, heavy weight, hand-engraved Crane's with a gold-embossed monogram, right? No way, says Karina.

How many invitations from weddings past do you have lying around your house? How long did they last after the couple's day was over? Unless you added the invite from your second cousin's third wedding to your scrapbook, it probably didn't survive the reception. Which is exactly the point of an invitation: It gets people to the wedding, and that's about it. If everyone's name is spelled correctly and the address, date, and time are right, it has done its job. So long as the invitations don't look like they were photocopied at work while the boss stepped out for a coffee, no one's going to care what you spent.

Before you even think of ordering invitations, you have to answer a lot of the big questions. As well as having finalized your guess list—a feat in itself—Karina suggests that you should be able to visualize the day and know your colors or your theme or just the ambiance you want to create. You're creating a marketing package, as much as you may love or hate the idea, so your stationery should reflect the kind of party you're throwing. Or not: Simple black and white cards are stylish without making it look like your wedding was planned by an ad agency. But sending out invitations embossed with seashells, then having a winter wedding, doesn't exactly give the impression that you guys have got it together.

Iona & Derrick
married: 30 years
wedding budget: $500

We had to invite our friends and our family, and they all came with their children and their babysitters and all. I mean, they just automatically assumed that everybody in the house was invited.

We met at a disco in Bombay named Hell, so you can say ours was a match made in hell!

❊ Getting It All on Paper

The invitation should contain the basic info: who, where, when, and what. The "who" is, of course, you, but it could also be your parents. Often **if the bride's parents are**

Guiding your guests to the right place on the right
day is only half the battle. Getting to the right number
is a chore in itself.

While you're loading up on paper, add "bring a tissue" to your to-do list.

paying for the wedding, their names will appear on the invite. **Skip this at your peril: Your parents know the rule.** If you're paying for the wedding, naturally the invitation should be from the two of you. Stationery stores will have suggestions for wording, and you can also find lots of ideas on the Internet, but really, anything that gets the point across and sets the tone is fine. If you're getting married in a picnic shelter, don't request the honor of their presence.

"Where" is the ceremony venue, and "when" is the date and time. So...make sure you've solidified these plans before ordering the invitations. You do not want to reprint these suckers. The "what" is also important. A short note at the bottom of the invitation, or a separate reception card, should indicate where and when the reception will be held, and what kind of reception it is. If you want to avoid grumbling stomachs (and grumbling guests), don't assume it's enough to say that the wedding's at seven and the reception will follow. Make sure you specify "cocktail reception" or "dinner and reception" or whatever it is, so guests know whether or not they should grab a burger on the way. If they will need to eat before the wedding, suggest some local restaurants to make it crystal clear.

Under some circumstances you may want to mention attire. Obviously, if you're going the black tie route, or would prefer that your guests come dressed as seventies sitcom characters, this is mandatory, but certain venues may require a nod to appropriate dress. For one wedding that took place in a field, the invitation stated, "The reception will be outdoors, so please dress accordingly." The intent was to let guests know they probably should bring a jacket and they might not want to wear stilettos. Several guests decided it meant shorts and Hawaiian shirts. Luckily, that was exactly the kind of atmosphere the couple was hoping for. If you just want to be sure people wear flat shoes for their own comfort but don't want your photos to include a guy sporting a "Vote for Pedro" T-shirt, be more specific.

The invitation should include the basic info, but it should also reflect the vibe you're going for. Include bits and pieces that capture the kind of couple you are: personal messages, song lyrics, photos, stuff like that. Whatever you want, with one exception: Never ever include where you are registered—or even worse, "Cash only, please."

In addition to the invitation, the basic stationery elements are the reply card and an envelope for each. **Save a bit of money right away by making the reply card a postcard, eliminating the cost of one envelope.** Request that guests respond no later than two weeks before the day. In addition to providing a spot for their response and whether or not

Invitation-Only

Before you start shopping for invites, know your theme. As the introduction to your wedding, invitations should set the tone and reflect your style.

they've wrangled a date, spare yourself the wrath of the vegans, the lactose-intolerant, the carb-counters—and your caterer—and provide a spot where they can indicate their dietary restriction or choice of entrée. Much easier for everyone than having to call the day before to make sure the buffet is kosher.

This is also a great place to state your policy on children. If you're welcoming them, make the wedding kid-friendly. Have food they will eat and dances they can join. It's a good idea to shell out an extra $200 for a sitter to watch the munchkins so they get some attention while their parents mingle and dance unencumbered. However, if you're hoping to avoid a room full of whirling dervishes hopped up on cake, and would prefer that people leave the kids at home, focus on the idea of limited space and blame it on the venue! Be warned, though, that this means absolutely no children: no flower girls, no ring bearers, and no adorable newborn nieces.

They look like little angels—until you add frosting, dry ice, and a lax curfew.

The cost for the basic package can range from $1 to $15 or more per person. The price will depend on paper stock, embellishments, method of printing, and number of colors. Be sure you both proof everything before the printer goes full steam ahead, and get a couple of trusted friends to look at everything too. Get

the ordering out of the way three to six months in advance so you have plenty of time to fix any embarrassing typos. Order more than you need, especially outer envelopes. You will screw a few up. Or your calligrapher will. Seriously—you can actually pay people with much better handwriting than you to address your invitations, but it will cost you. If you're not willing to spend on that, enlist the help of a friend or parent with great handwriting to help you address them, invite your wedding party to help you stuff them, and buy several bottles of wine to make the drudgery of addressing, stuffing, and stamping a hundred or more envelopes into a party. Send out invitations! (How ironic.) Order pizza! Throw on "Muriel's Wedding!" Anything to trick your slave labor into helping you. Stamp the reply cards or envelopes as well as the outer envelopes, and mail the invitations about six to eight weeks before the wedding.

❊ The Complete Package

There are many other paper elements you can add, and having them all done on the same stationery gives your wedding a cohesive look. First of all, there are save the date cards, otherwise known as "Find a Date" or "Prepare Your Excuse" cards. If many of your guests will have to travel a great distance, or if you're planning your wedding for a time of year when lots of people go on vacation, such as August, consider warning them well in advance. If you only send them to guests who will have to travel, be aware that word will get out to family and friends who don't receive them, and confusion and

Give your guests lots of clues to finding their seat. Seating charts, escort cards, place cards, and a friendly face at the door cut down on foyer chaos.

Instead of a bland guestbook full of "best wishes," provide cards
on which your guests write their suggestions for a successful marriage.

recrimination will reign. Save the date cards can be very affordable, ranging from $1 to $5 each, so you might as well send them to everyone. A good time to do this is about six months in advance. However, if you're still fighting with your parents over the guest list and the wedding's four months away, don't bother with save the date cards. Just email guests who will have to travel.

Other elements you should consider are:

❋ **Reception cards:** Got extra cash, or elaborate directions from the ceremony to the reception venue? Put your reception info on a separate insert. This is also handy if you're inviting some guests to the reception but not the ceremony, as you can just send them this card.

❋ **Travel information:** Adding an insert with a map and hotel listings is important if you don't want dozens of people calling to ask where they should stay. To cut down on costs, include travel inserts only in the invites of out-of-town guests.

❋ **Ceremony programs:** Some places of worship will offer to include these with the cost of the service, but a lot of people do their own so they can add a personal touch. And so they'll match, of course. Tell your story, write fun bios of the wedding party— give your guests something to read while your limos are stuck in traffic.

❋ **Thank you cards:** If you order thank you cards at the same time as your invitations, you can usually get them at a reduced cost as part of the package. It's also good to get them early enough for shower gifts.

And there are the more unusual items like rain cards (which indicate where an outdoor wedding will be relocated if the weather doesn't cooperate), within-the-ribbon cards (something of a VIP pass to the first few rows), escort cards (strangely, not a way for

Got a lot of VIPs? Provide them with within-the-ribbon cards, so they know they should sit at the front.

unattached guests to find a date; they actually indicate where each guest is to sit), matchbooks (a throwback to another era—or a dangerous way to keep bored guests occupied)...the list goes on forever. Don't feel you have to go overboard on the auxiliary stuff—remember, most of this will just get thrown out. Karina knows of one bride who insisted on using the same paper stock as Queen Elizabeth. The bill for her stationery came to $7,500! And most of the guests didn't even bother to take a ceremony program.

❋ Running Your Own Print Shop

At the same time, if you're trying to rein in your budget, don't go too far. Your guests will know that you photocopied your invitations. (And your boss may get suspicious.) Invitations are a great place to cut down on costs without it looking like you did. You don't need raised print to pull off an elegant appearance. Limit the number of colors. One or two ink colors are cheaper than four. And forgo inner envelopes and bows. They're not just unnecessary expenses. The heavier the paper stock and the more embellishments and inserts, the more postage will cost.

Many couples start their search for invitations at stationery stores, where you can flip through giant books with hundreds of samples. **The best place to find deals on all things paper is the Internet, although you may find local artists who offer unique stationery at really good prices.** Small printers will have booths at bridal shows and will be listed on wedding websites that cater to your region. **Another budget-friendly option is to print your own.** Office supply stores often have wedding invitation kits that include invitations, reply cards, and envelopes in one package. If you have access to a laser printer, these can be very affordable and still elegant. If you're not using a kit, make sure you buy plenty of extra stationery for all you'll waste figuring out how to fit it in the printer.

Believe it or not, there are times when an email invitation is appropriate, according to Karina. If you're planning an environmentally friendly wedding, a shotgun wed-

> **KARINA ON ALTERNATIVES TO THE GUESTBOOK:** *No one writes anything interesting in guestbooks. And ones that aren't tacky are expensive. The best alternatives are cards that guests write wishes on and drop in a glass vase; a photo with a large matte that guests sign; or a photo album with pictures of the couple and room for guests to sign. My favorite is to take a Polaroid of every guest, have them sign the bottom part of the picture, and mount the pictures in an album.*

ding (you need at least six to eight weeks for paper invitations), or if most guests are on email, you can consider electronic invitations. Evite.com even has wedding templates, so apparently you're not the only one considering this option. The bonus is that the replies come in a lot quicker. Of course, it also means that any inappropriate comments posted by your friends will be seen by your tech-savvy great-aunt, your priest, your father-in-law's business partner....

Please sign the matte with the pens provided.

Another guestbook alternative is also a work of art: a photo framed with a large matte for your guests to sign.

Weddings with a Conscience

All those felled trees for the sake of pure-white invitations,
programs, and thank-you cards got you down? Reduce
your strappy-sandal carbon print with eco-friendly options,
such as live favors and high-quality fake flowers.

Think carefully about going "green" unless you have plenty of it. Organic food and fair-trade flowers cost much more than their chemical-laden, labor-exploitive alternatives. That said, here are some tips that are budget-friendly as well as eco-friendly.

1 Use recycled paper or rice paper for your invitations.

2 Better yet, don't send paper invitations. **Email or phone your guests, and set up a website to provide them with all the information they'll need.**

3 Step away from the stretch Hummer limo. No one will see you pull up in it anyway. Use a compact car, rent a hybrid, or travel the old-fashioned way in a horse and buggy (provided they don't have to travel far to get to you).

4 Forgo the useless knickknacks. Give live favors, such as tree seedlings, bulbs, seed packets, or lucky bamboo, and wrap them in burlap or unbleached muslin.

5 Or forgo favors entirely, and make a donation to a charity on behalf of your guests.

6 Donate any leftover food to a shelter. Many will have restrictions on accepting perishable foods, so make arrangements with your caterer in advance.

7 Give your mother's wedding gown a second turn. And not by wearing it: Cut it up to make your flower girl's dress, ribbons for bouquets, and your handkerchief. **Just make sure you check with her first.**

8 Once you're done with them, donate your centerpieces to a seniors' residence. That should stop your guests from fighting over them.

9 Buy your dress from a socially-conscious store like The Bride's Project in Toronto (www.thebridesproject.com) or the Making Memories Breast Cancer Foundation (www.makingmemories.org), which donates all proceeds from its used gowns to making wishes come true for cancer patients. Or donate your dress. **And since your bridesmaids aren't really going to wear those dresses again, suggest they donate theirs too.**

10 If your budget allows, hire an organic caterer and serve fair-trade coffee.

DRESSES and TRESSES

It's your big day, the one you've been dreaming of for a couple years or a few decades, so

naturally you want to look like the supermodel you are. Ironically, you'll also be completely

stressed, which means you'll be fighting ragged nails, dark circles under your eyes, and what-

ever else your treacherous body tends to spring on you when you need it the least.

Stress is a big part of being a bride. You may swear up and down you're not that kind

of bride, that you won't flip out over little things like the best man's decision to wear white

socks, but even the most easygoing girl reaches the end of her rope eventually. If you're a bit of a control freak to begin with, you probably won't be surprised by this kind of reaction. If you aren't, don't worry. It's perfectly normal. As long as you don't make tantrums a regular part of your routine, one or two will help clear the air.

Your wedding day is not the time to let last-minute glitches get to you, and there really is no need to waste waterproof mascara on situations you can't control. Hopefully

> **ALLISTER ON GETTING GORGEOUS:** *My number one tip is to start your wedding day with a massage. You'll start the day in a state of bliss. Have the hairdresser and makeup artist come to you. Pay a little extra to have the makeup artist stick around until after the ceremony for touch-ups before photos. You're being pampered all day, so enjoy yourself!*

you've delegated problem-solving duties to your generous support network. All those people who offered to lend a hand long ago will be thrilled to be an important part of your day, and since there's not much damage they can do now, don't be afraid to ask for help. Now you can focus on making this day about you.

❧ You've Got the Look

Put a lot of thought into the look you want, but also trust the professionals you've hired to do your hair and makeup. Allister sees too many brides aim for the unattainable rather than work with their natural beauty. Face the facts: If you're a red-head, you are never going to look like Halle Berry, and if you try, you'll just look weird. However, if you like the way her eyes are done in a certain picture, bring it to your makeup consultation and

Be sure to wear waterproof mascara, Ice Queen. You never
know what's gonna tug at your heart strings.

a good artist will be happy to adapt the look to suit you. Copy bits and pieces from looks you like, but don't expect the whole thing. As near-sighted as your grandma might be, she should at least be able to tell it's you she's watching go up the aisle.

You'd really have to try hard to blow the budget on your hair. Unless you absolutely must fly in some fabulous celebrity stylist from L.A., you'll probably visit your regular hairdresser. Most women are not comfortable with just any stranger doing their hair, no matter who the hairdresser has "done," and their wedding day is no exception. So if you have a hairdresser you trust, keep trusting him. Book a consultation with him about a month in advance of the wedding. Take a picture of your dress and clippings of ideas you like, as well as any accessories you want to use.

Meeting the deadline is crucial for everyone on your wedding day. Don't forget to fit in your bridesmaids when scheduling hair and makeup.

If you have a veil, take it so he can figure out how to incorporate it into your hairstyle. Many brides opt for simple styles, which are easier to put up with on a hot day than some massive beehive, or just leave their hair down, which is cheaper than an up-do. Your everyday hair can look special with a few rhinestone pins or flowers thrown in. And with a professional who knows what products to add, it'll look fresh and frizz-free all day.

You also want to consider your bridesmaids' hair. Your wedding day schedule may require that everyone visit the same salon, or it may allow them to visit their own hairdresser. Work this out in advance so they're not stuck doing their own hair at the last minute. And you can give them suggestions, not demands—only evil dictators require everyone to grow their hair the same length and wear identical up-dos.

Up or Down? The Choice is Yours

It's nearly impossible to spend your entire budget on your hair, so why not have it done professionally? After all, there are two important things you'll take away from your wedding: the memories... and the photos.

No Traffic Jams!

Your wedding day can be peaceful and comfortable with a little planning. Avoid running around and make your home the center of activity by having your hair stylist and makeup artist come to you.

❀ Beauty Queen, Ice Queen...or Priscilla, Queen of the Desert?

Many brides decide to cut costs by doing their own makeup. Allister advises against this. If you truly want to look your best, your everyday makeup just won't do. A professional makeup artist will do whatever you want, only better. If you're a natural girl and just want to bring it up a level, a professional will know how far to go, and will be able to use cosmetics you're not used to. If you're used to a lot of makeup and want to go really dramatic, she'll keep you from resembling a drag queen. Find artists by asking your hairdresser or other vendors, such as bridal salons, for referrals. **Most makeup artists charge about $75 for a consultation and between $150 and $400 per person for the actual sitting; the price per person should go down if your bridesmaids also get their makeup done.** Offer the option to them—and to your mom and mother-in-law, too—or treat them as a thank you gift. To save money, find an aspiring makeup artist who will come to your home for around $25 per person. Makeup schools will have bulletin boards posting advertisements from students, or the receptionists can provide you with names. Or you can even go to the mall on the day of your wedding and get a free cosmetic-counter makeover—if you dare!

Book a consultation with your makeup artist so you know what you're getting. Schedule it for the same day as your hair consultation so your makeup artist can create a look that will suit the hairstyle you'll have on your wedding day. Take along a picture of your dress and any clippings that interest you. The consultation should take about two hours, and the artist should try different looks until you're both happy. If you're not used to wearing a lot of makeup, the consultation can be a bit of a shock. Take a step back from the mirror and imagine what you'll look like from the other side of the room, especially in a white dress that may otherwise wash you out in photos. A professional makeup artist knows to compensate for these factors.

The makeup artist should come to your home on your wedding day, and if she's doing the whole wedding party, she should do you last so you'll look fresh. Ask her to stick around until after the ceremony so she can refresh your makeup before pictures are taken. And wear waterproof mascara, Ice Queen. You never know what's gonna tug at your heart strings.

🌷 Your Grand Entrance

When you walk down that aisle, heads should turn. Literally—if you've planned the music right, the guests should get the idea and turn around. But naturally, you want people to gasp when they see you—for all the right reasons. The guy at the other end of the aisle should be pretty impressed too. Thankfully, finding that "wow" dress isn't all about big budgets and designer labels.

Or maybe it can be about designer labels even if you don't have the designer budget, says Heidi. Fashion moves slowly, so the pick-up skirts now worn by au courant brides were worn by celebrities two years ago and appeared on runways two years before that. They'll probably be worn by brides for the next two years too. So definitely consider sample sales and discount racks. Unless the salon still has stock from the eighties, no one will be

Lillian & Craig
married: 23 years
wedding budget: $20,000

I always thought she was beautiful, and just more outstanding in the white dress when she was walking down the aisle, so she really did stand out. I didn't notice the other people around her that much.

He was a good groom because he just wanted to make me happy, so he just let me do what I wanted, and would say, "Okay, okay."

Maria & Scott

Maria wanted the perfect wedding—at any cost. She worked with a personal trainer (although not with Scott's budget) to get into the dress of her dreams.

able to tell that your dress is four seasons old. If you really want a couture dress, you may find one for up to 50% off.

Trunk sales are another good way to find designer gowns at discount prices. Before a designer's line hits stores, designers visit salons to show their upcoming wares. Special deals are given to the salons to encourage them to buy, and they often pass this discount on to you. Check designer and bridal salon websites for notices on upcoming shows. **Many salons have trunk shows after a bridal show, so look for notices at their booths.**

You've bought your invitations, favors, and "Bride" and "Groom" flip-flops on the Internet—why not your dress? Here are a few things Heidi would like you to keep in mind before you click away on that unbelievably affordable Reem Acra that's just your size: It's going to look completely different on you than it does on the model in the picture, so you're bound to be disappointed. Even if you try a dress on in a salon, then buy the same one on eBay, it will likely have been altered to fit the original owner, and

HEIDI ON PUTTING THE SALES STAFF TO WORK: *The worst thing you can do when dress shopping is to go with a list of things you don't want. Instead, tell the staff what you like, what you normally wear, what kind of person you are, and their job will be much easier.*

there's a good chance the material and construction are sub-par, or there are stains or tears you weren't warned of. If you're going to buy on consignment, do so locally so you can see exactly what you're getting. A "green" option that can also help you save money is to buy a used dress. Some stores that sell used wedding dresses donate the proceeds to charity, so you'll be doubly virtuous. Bridesmaids should also consider this option. Or ask your mom if you can wear her dress. In either case, be prepared to spend a hundred dollars or so on alterations.

❀ Dress Rehearsal

Remember, this is the most important shopping excursion of your life! Or at least the most expensive. Plan accordingly. The mega stores can be veritable battlefields, with brides fighting over dresses, change rooms, and staff. Small boutiques may have a smaller selection, but they can give you the attention you need. And don't bring an entourage with you. A five-person panel does not mean five sources of positive feedback and confirmation that you've found just the right dress. It means five wildly divergent sets of expectations and opinions. You'll never make them all happy, so take one friend whose taste you respect. If that person isn't your maid of honor or your mom, don't worry. They can come to your first fitting.

That's right; don't assume you have to take your mother. If your relationship is antagonistic or competitive, or she clearly doesn't approve of your sense of style, it can only lead to disaster. Heidi has seen too many brides leave her salon in tears because their mothers belittled them. In one particularly heinous incident, a bride tried on a dress that looked stunning on her, but her mother shot it down, made her try on a plain dress, and

The perfect dress looks different on the rack than on you. Step outside your comfort zone—you never know what you'll find!

told her that was the one she was getting. Then Psycho Mom snuck to the cashier and asked for the first dress in a different color—for her mother-of-the-bride dress! If this sounds at all plausible to you, leave Mom at home. If you still need that mother-daughter wedding dress experience, bring her to a fitting, when it's far too late for her to interfere.

Fortunately, salon staff are trained to be much more supportive (if a tad handsy). But only if you let them help you. Try anything and everything at first, and slowly narrow your scope…many brides-to-be are happily surprised when that oh-so-frumpy dress they would never have chosen to try transforms into the perfectly smashing dress!

Flip through some bridal magazines and bring some ideas, but don't do too much research. What you like in magazines may not look right on you, so be open-minded. The staff have lots of experience picking dresses for your body type, coloring, and personality. Before you go, though, check the rules at your ceremony venue. Catholic churches, for instance, often forbid bare shoulders and excess cleavage. If yours does, but you want to go strapless anyway, get a shawl or jacket. At one wedding Heidi attended, the priest actually stopped a bare-shouldered bride as she came down the

aisle and forced her to wear the groom's jacket. The bride was in tears for the entire ceremony, the pictures were ruined…and all could have been saved with a $40 shawl.

As an aside, mysterious evil people decided that wedding dresses should be two sizes smaller than normal clothes, so be prepared for a shock. Once you've picked a dress, the salon staff will measure your chest, waist, and hips and determine your size from a chart provided by the manufacturer. The chart is wrong, of course, but it is also your key to the perfect gown, so just let it slide this one time. Barring a wardrobe malfunction, no one will actually see the label anyway, so your secret is safe.

🌷 Nice Day for a Petal Pink Wedding

Wedding dresses can be a lot more creative than the traditional white pouf. More designers are adding colored accents, and even colored crinolines. Diamond white is becoming popular—a shade that's more flattering to pale complexions than stark white, yet isn't quite ivory. Dresses have become more bride-friendly, with innovations such as built-in corsetry, flexible hoops (a lot more comfortable than scratchy crinoline, but the same effect), and light-weight taffeta. Yup, taffeta. Not just for the prom anymore.

Your wedding celebration is about sharing the love: try to find a few quiet moments with family.

Something Borrowed, Something Blue

Accessories can bring your whole look together, but they don't have to break the bank or dazzle with opulence. Simple touches like satin sashes can add a dash of color. Fancy shoes are great, but if no one will see them, consider getting a cheaper, more comfortable pair. Buy a matching cover-up to ward off over-enthusiastic air conditioning or disapproving officiants. Otherwise, you might be stuck borrowing Aunt Mabel's moth-eaten fox stole at the last minute.

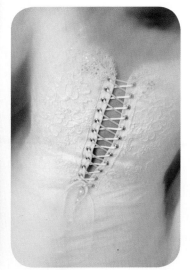

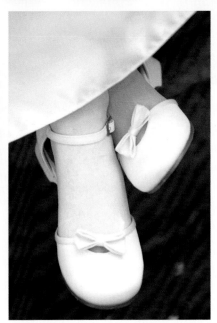

Pitch the bouquet toss for a Turkish tradition: Have single guests autograph the soles of your shoes. The name that's faded the most when the party's over will marry next.

A dress can take up to eight months to manufacture, and you should allow two months after that for alterations, so Heidi recommends that you start shopping a year in advance. You should also start early if you're having your dress made by a dressmaker who promises to make you the perfect Vera Wang knock-off. **Expect to spend about 5 to 10% of your budget on your outfit, including accessories. The average price range for a dress is $800 to $1,500.** When you go to the salon, tell them your price range (and allow yourself a little wiggle room), and only try on dresses in this range.

When you go back for fittings, take your accessories. Be sure to wear suitable underwear so you can get the full effect without distracting, blue bra straps. Don't worry about panty lines with your bias-cut sheath gown. Flesh-toned laser cut thongs are a girl's best friend.

You may want to set aside a couple hundred dollars, at least, for accessories—shoes, jewelery, veil, tiara, gloves, that obligatory garter for some guy's rear-view mirror—but you can also cut costs in this area. If your dress is floor length, no one's going to see your Jimmy Choos, so your shoes might as well be cheap and comfy. Borrowing a veil and jewelery is a great way to incorporate your friends and family into your attire.

Of course, if you absolutely must have a genuine Vera Wang, expect to pay $10,000. And expect no one to realize that you're wearing a Vera Wang. The best dress isn't the most expensive; it's the one that suits you the most.

Looking Fabulous from Head to Toe

Looking great isn't just about the dress, the tux, and the perfect hair. Here are some tips for pampering your inner Beauty King or Queen without breaking the bank.

1 Girls, fit in some quality spa time with your bridal party a day or two before the wedding. It doesn't have to be a major investment—just a night at home with a couple of bottles of nail polish, a couple of bottles of wine, and some cheesy movies will put you in the right frame of mind for the coming days.

2 Guys, why not try a manicure? Don't worry: No polish will sully your manly nails; they'll just be shaped and buffed. A facial is also not out of the question. No one has to know, and you won't regret it. Just make sure you get it done a couple of weeks in advance (girls too) so any adverse reactions have time to clear up.

3 Don't panic on your wedding day, though: Use Visine to "get the red out" of untimely skin eruptions.

4 If you want your skin to look fabulous without shelling out for a facial, cut dairy out of your diet a month or more before your wedding, and make sure you drink lots and lots of water.

5 If you haven't tried waxing before, and you want to do it for your wedding, start going a few months in advance. That way, you'll know if your skin will react, and you'll have an idea of how far in advance you should get it done. If you bruise easily, you may want to get waxed a week in advance; if your hair grows quickly, maybe a couple of days before.

6 If you color your hair, touch it up two weeks before the wedding—enough time to fix any mistakes, but not so much time that your roots show. If you don't color your hair, two weeks before your wedding is not the time to start.

7 Hair extensions are an option if you want more volume, or you want layers or length but don't have time. However, they can cost anywhere from $450 to $2,000, depending on the number and kind (synthetic or real). Make sure you get them far enough in advance to formulate a Plan B, though; they're braided in very tightly, so some people get serious headaches and end up ripping them out.

8 Speaking of headaches, try a bit of Gatorade if your head starts to pound from all the pressure. Or if you had a little too much fun at the rehearsal dinner.

9 Remember to eat something before the ceremony. So many couples feel ill or faint when they don't take the time to relax and have a snack. You're not going to gain weight at this point, so quit worrying and eat something!

10 Make sure your makeup artist leaves you a little lip color and powder so you can do touch-ups long after he's gone.

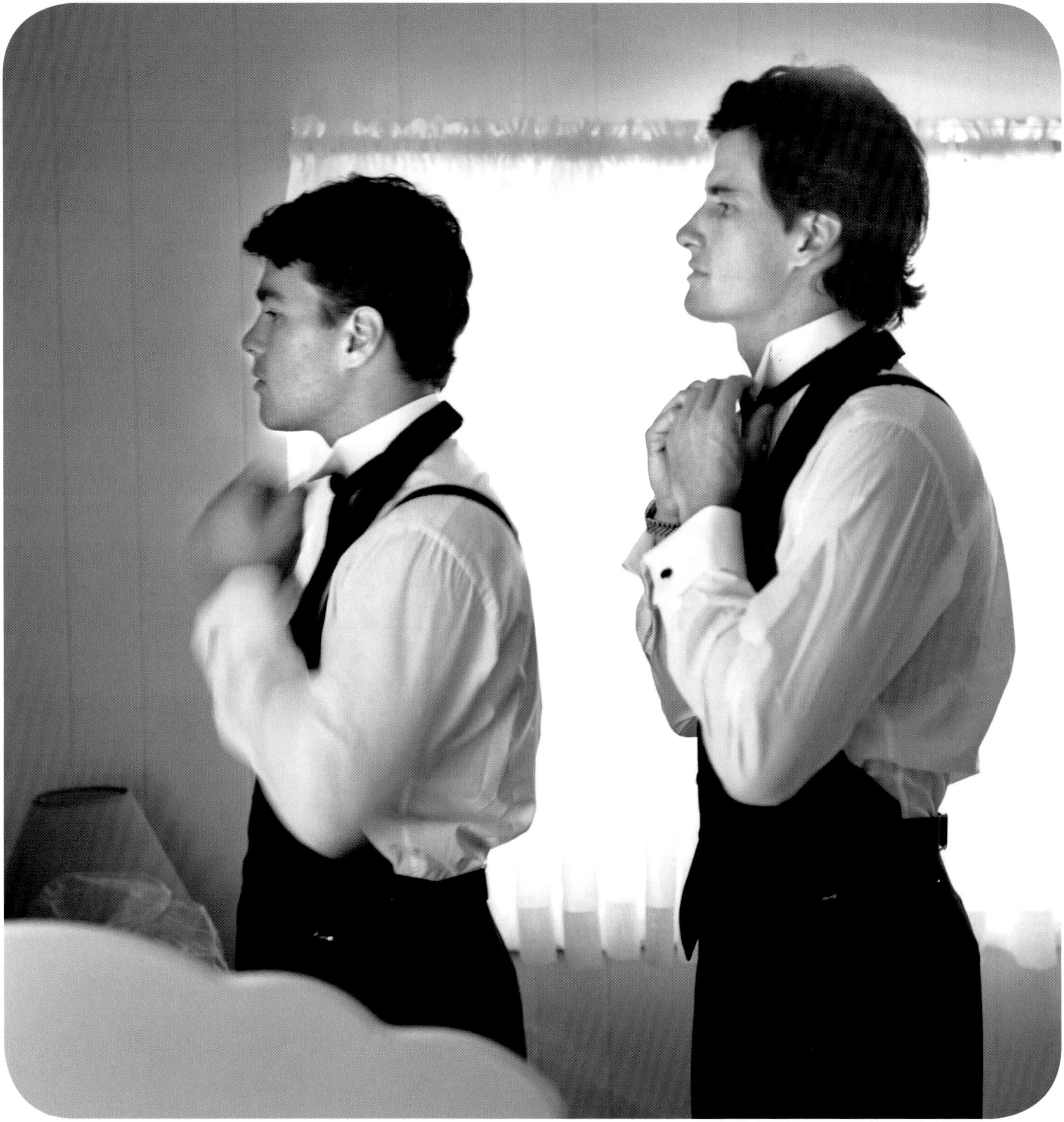

The *TUX MANUAL*

The days of the uninvolved groom are over, as you're well aware if you're the groom. Wow, you're reading a wedding book? That's okay—everybody's doing it. As we become inundated with the smallest details of the latest celebrity wedding, what guy wouldn't get excited about incorporating Tom Cruise's heel lifts or Kid Rock's yacht into his own wedding day? Grooms can sometimes feel lost, left out, or in the way during the process of wedding planning. But it's your day too, so get involved. You're setting the stage for the rest of your life together, so it's a great chance to work as a team and practice the art of compromise.

✿ Party of Two

Compromise is the key to a good wedding, as much as it is to a good marriage, so be prepared to discuss your ideas, but also be prepared to negotiate. The idea for a wrestling-

> **HEIDI ON TAKING IT TO THE NET:** *A wedding website can provide all the details your guests are dying to know, so you don't have to answer the same questions over and over again. Use it to tell the story of how you met, provide links to your gift registries, introduce the wedding party, and provide directions and sightseeing information.*

themed cake may have seemed great when you dreamed it up at the bar last night, but you'll need a convincing argument if you want it to stand a chance against the cake she's been dreaming of since she was little.

If you don't know where to start, show some interest in what your bride is doing, and contribute to the areas where your interests and skills would be a natural fit. Take charge of music, or design a website, or plan the honeymoon. Be responsible for the wedding rings: Pick a jeweler, schedule a shopping trip, and get them engraved. Or just give her a break from the whole planning process by taking her to dinner every once in a while. Don't become a walking checkbook. Combine strengths and allow each person to do what he or she does best. That's what your marriage should be about, after all.

Gaynor & Tab
married: 28 years
wedding budget:
$5,000

What did I think of Gaynor in her dress? Um, not too many guys as lucky as I am on a day like this.

And you looked pretty hot yourself, Honey.

Think of how impressed your best buds will be when you tell them you picked out the flowers! Kidding—but a little involvement won't hurt your rep.

⬢ Clothes Make the Man

Just as some girls dream of their wedding gown when they're little, some guys dream of being James Bond. If you're that guy, now's your chance. But you actually have other options, so only rent a tuxedo if you really want to. Wedding shows will usually have tuxedo rental vendors on hand, but they're just the same people you ordered your prom tux from, so they shouldn't be hard to find. If you want to limit the amount of time you spend in a store, you can usually check out your options in brochures or on websites. There are lots of options for different styles, collars, and accessories, so keep an open mind, but take into consideration the type of wedding you're having. Just because you can rent a morning suit, cane, and top hat doesn't mean you should. For accessories, consider a tie rather than a bow tie, a pocket square or a vest rather than a cummerbund, and subdued colors like silver or gray rather than aquamarine to match the bridesmaids' dresses. Try the tux on well in advance so you're sure you're happy with how it looks. Arrange to pick it up a couple of days before the wedding, and try everything on again at the store to make sure it still fits. If you're leaving for the honeymoon right after the wedding, get someone reliable to return the tux to the rental shop.

⬢ Cutting the Bow Ties that Bind

Despite their popularity, tuxedos are rarely appropriate, says David Vallee. Traditionally, grooms are not supposed to be any more

Your morning routine may take all of 10 minutes, but a tuxedo presents a whole new set of challenges. Give yourself plenty of time.

formally dressed than the guests, and tuxes aren't supposed to be worn until after sundown, so unless the wedding's black tie and in the evening, you don't need to go the rental tux route. Plus, why wear someone else's clothes on your wedding day? What you wear should be as formal or as informal as the wedding itself. A classic black suit is appropriate for almost any occasion. If the wedding's informal, forgo the tie and open your collar (and just your collar, Slick—one button only). For a wedding on a beach or at a cottage, a light-colored linen suit or a navy blazer with khaki shorts looks great and ensures you won't roast in the heat. Wearing something with cultural significance (if it's your culture, of course) is always a great idea. Finally, here's your chance to wear a kilt! But please resist the urge to go commando underneath. People will be eating, you know.

The best thing about the no-tux option is that you may already have your outfit in your closet, and if not, you can buy it at a reasonable cost. You can get a

All in the Details

Accessories let you express your personal style, even when you're stuck in the same old penguin suit.

new suit for the price of a rental, so why wouldn't you? If you and your groomsmen will be buying suits, find a retailer who might give you a deal on several suits. Be willing to compromise on the style so that everyone can get a suit that's perfect for them. David suggests a classic black suit, white shirt, gray tie, and silver cufflinks. Together they

> **DAVID VALLEE ON RING VERSUS BLING:** *Wait a second before you splurge on that gold chain and pinky ring to give your outfit some extra dash. Once again, less is more. All a man really needs in terms of jewelery are a watch, cufflinks, and the wedding ring. If you're looking to impress, just upgrade these items.*

look formal, and can be reasonably affordable. After the wedding, the jacket and shirt will look great with jeans. If your bride is stuck for gift ideas, suggest that she buy you the cufflinks. Starting at $150, she can get a pair of sterling silver cufflinks that will last forever. And your son could wear them on his wedding day. Now that's classy.

⚙ Rental Shoes Are for Bowling

Whatever you do, says David, don't rent shoes. Rental shoes are usually poorly made. Not to mention that someone else has worn them. If you don't have a pair of classic lace-ups, spend about $100 to $200 on a new pair. **A good pair of shoes will last a long time if you maintain them well.** Wear them a bit before the wedding to avoid bloodshed and an awkward first dance. There's a temptation for brides and grooms to have everything pristine and new for their wedding day, but if it's new, it's unfamiliar and possibly painful. Your wedding should be a reflection of your life, not your fantasy life. With one exception: your fantasy socks. Splurge on a new pair of black socks. Your bride will not be impressed when you strip down to holey old socks on your wedding night. And by the way, there are absolutely no circumstances in which it is acceptable to wear white socks with black pants.

❀ Why Does the Bride Get All the Fun?

Of course, if you're a flamboyant guy, you're bound to want to stand out a little. David knows one groom who ordered a custom-made suit complete with diamanté detail and a purple scarf. He probably spent as much on his outfit as the bride spent on hers—and guests were left with the impression that he was competing with her for their attention. David believes that male beauty is a subdued and discreet quality. If you want to be colorful and outrageous, wear a powder blue tux to the rehearsal party. But skip the matching cummerbund and bow tie on your wedding day. The only guy who can get away with that look is under five years old.

The bride's not the only star of the show. Grooms should dress to impress too.

❂ If *Maxim* Says It's Okay…

There are a few things you can do to look slick without going totally metrosexual. Get your hair cut a few weeks before the wedding so it's tidy but not freshly cut. Closer to the wedding, make sure you take care of any other unsightly hair—you know: nose, ears, knuckles, stuff like that. Clip your nails and make sure they're clean. If you're feeling a bit adventurous and have some extra cash, it's perfectly normal for guys to get manicures and facials. Don't worry; they won't make you wear nail polish. A manicurist will clean, shape, and buff your nails to a discreet shine. If you get a facial, go a couple of weeks before the wedding. Not only will you look like a new man, but a spa visit usually involves a beautiful woman taking pains to make sure you are pampered. You just might like it.

Your groomsmen will stand by you on your wedding day. Even if you get a facial.

Wedding books seem to have plenty of to-do lists for brides, but rarely do they tell grooms what they should know. Here's a list of things to keep in mind.

1 **Remove something from your bride's to-do list for the wedding preparations.** Make it a *big* thing like the budget or the registry, not something small like picking the dessert or adding your poker buddies to the bloated guest list.

2 Because you likely bought the engagement ring, you know where to go to buy the wedding bands, especially if they are part of a set. **But consult with your bride on her wedding band before you buy...**or if not her, her sister, best friend, or her mother should be able to help. For a few extra bucks—and a reminder for future anniversaries—engrave the wedding date inside the bands.

3 **Buy your shoes at least one month ahead of time to wear them in . . . and then hide them.** Otherwise your meddling friends may be inspired to write "HELP" on the bottom of one and "ME" on the other.

4 **Ensure your suit or tux fits perfectly.** "Look, Grandpa wore floods at his wedding" is not what you want to hear from your grandchildren in years to come.

5 Romance your fiancée. As the wedding day draws close, your bride will be stressed. **Find surprising ways to keep her laughing and madly in love with you.**

6 Honor the Boy Scout tradition and BE PREPARED. **If you are not a "list" type of guy, become one.** Compare notes with your fiancée to make sure you're not duplicating or forgetting anything. Your line is "I do," not "I forgot."

7 Don't have your bachelor party the night before, and limit your consumption on the day of the wedding. **There will be other days to drink; you need all your senses in sharp focus on this particular one.**

8 **This is likely one of the most stressful days of your fiancée's life, so don't take anything personally.** (You think it's bad now—just wait until you're in the delivery room for the first time.)

9 You'll have some free time on your wedding day, so why not play a round of golf? It'll take longer than normal to get ready today, especially if

you and your groomsmen are wearing tuxes for the first time. **Keep it to nine holes so you're not rushed.**

10 **Steal a moment** when she least expects it to pull her in to a private area, look her in the eyes, and tell her you are the happiest man on earth.

TO EAT *is* DIVINE

From the point of view of your guests, the meal is the grand pay-off for spending $200 on a

set of towels they'll never see again. But your options aren't just limited to sit-down versus

buffet, or chicken parmigiana versus beef tenderloin. Depending on the level of formality you

want—and, of course, your budget—you can feed the hungry masses any number of ways.

Many couples are surprised to learn that they don't need to have a four course sit-down dinner.

Cheaper options abound, such as a buffet, barbecue, luncheon, or cocktail party, and might

be the perfect fit for your particular party.

❋ Sit Down, Stand Up, Bite Bite Bite!

Don't feel like you're tied to the traditional, says David Vallee. Do what feels right (short of asking your guests to contribute to a potluck dinner). And if you can't do what you want on your budget, adjust your expectations—and the length of your guest list.

Buffet-style dinners don't necessarily have to resemble a trip to Ponderosa. Food stations add creativity and a higher level of quality to the experience of serving yourself. A beef carving station, sushi tray, made-to-order pasta station, or dessert table are all great options for dine-around meals. If the food could just as easily be served to your guests at their tables, a buffet seems like a bit of a cop-out. Besides, it's not that much cheaper. You still need staff to serve food at the buffet and to clear dishes, and there are often more rentals required: more dishes and cutlery for second helpings, and more tables and linen for the actual buffet. While food stations will encourage variety and socializing, sit-down meals should be all about relaxing and being pampered. Make the choice according to the kind of wedding you want, and then get creative with the costs (tips ahead!).

❋ Chicken or Fish?

The standard banquet hall fare is pretty predictable, and not exactly stellar. Hotel food is also limited, but usually better quality. Very rarely will they let you bring in outside food, and if they do, they'll probably charge you for the privilege. So if you opt for that kind of venue, your choices will be limited. Which could be a blessing—you've already got enough decisions to make! If you want to bring in specialty food like sushi, better wine, or your own cake, try to negotiate your way out of the extra charges. Unless there is a lot of demand for your specific day, make it a condition of sealing the deal.

No room in the budget for the formal dinner you dream of? Be ruthless with that guest list.

Banquet halls make it easy to feed your guests, but caterers allow you to serve exactly what you want, wherever you want.

Great Nibbles
Buffet-style meals
should provide a
culinary adventure, not
an excuse to cut costs.

If you live in a small town, you probably know the reputations of the local caterers. They usually have one or two dishes they're known for, and they charge really low rates. If you want something more avant-garde than a home-cooked meal, you're likely to be disappointed. Caterers might agree to do something out of their comfort zone just to get the job. But listen to what they're trying to sell you, because that's probably what they do best. Restaurants that cater are also limited in what they can do, but for different reasons. The logistics of serving 80 people at once are different from serving 20 tables of four over the course of a few hours, so they aren't as skilled as exclusive caterers. **However, having your favorite restaurant cater your wedding is usually affordable, and, if it sticks to its specialties, a pretty safe bet.**

In urban areas, you have the option of fine-food caterers. If you can afford it, this is your best option. They're experts at preparing high-quality food for a large number of people, they're able to create unique meals, and they're experienced event planners. Many specialize in specific cultural or religious cuisines, which makes it a lot easier to get exactly what you want. **Culinary schools often provide inexpensive fine-food catering.** The level of quality might not be quite as good as that of a professional, but the students have a vested interest in providing excellent food and service. As a bonus, the programs often have no profit margin and are therefore extremely affordable.

✳ Finding Your Foodie

One way to find a caterer is to ask your venue. Non-traditional venues such as galleries and museums will probably have a list of caterers who are used to operating in their specific space, so they'll do a better job than some guy who has no idea what to expect. Another way is through word of mouth. Ask friends, family, and other vendors—such as your wedding planner—for referrals. If you haven't hired a wedding planner, a caterer can often fulfill parts of that job, as many include event planning as part of their service. They may not help you with everything—don't expect them to go dress shopping with you—but they're a great source of referrals and can help make sure everything runs smoothly on the day.

Booking a caterer is one thing that you can put off, says David. In fact, if you're not too concerned about the menu or the cost, you can book it as late as two weeks in advance. That wasn't a recommendation; it's

Sandra & Len
married: 41 years
wedding budget:
$3,000

My oldest brother Will came up and hugged me and said, "Sandra, be happy and safe." He turned to Len and said, "If you don't take good care of her, I'll knock your block off."

Hey, my sister said the same thing to me.

A tent lacks key amenities your caterer needs, namely water and power. Luckily, both can be rented.

just nice to know where your safety nets are. The caterer doesn't need to know your exact numbers until a week before the wedding, because most won't order food until a few days before. However, if you're really picky about food, want a specific caterer,

> **DAVID VALLEE ON FREE FOOD:** *Sample meals are the bane of a caterer's existence. Many couples turn the search for a caterer into a month-long movable feast. If you really don't know what to expect (or if you're certifiably, post-dress-shopping starving), ask for a sample—but only once you've picked your caterer.*

or live in a small town where there are only a couple of vendors, you probably want to get it done early.

Get a detailed quote as soon as you've made your decision. The quote should include taxes, labor, rentals, and gratuities, if any, and the total cost per person. David warns that surgically attacking the quote to fit your budget is more trouble than it's worth. If the caterer suggests a certain number of staff, asking that the number be cut by one just to save money will affect your guests' experience more than your wallet. Generally, one waiter can serve about 20 people at a banquet, so you should have roughly one for every two tables. On the other hand, if you've got the bucks and you want everyone to be served simultaneously, à la Buckingham Palace or a state dinner, it's fine to request more staff.

Don't dare skimp on servers to save cash. A good guideline is one server for two tables; any fewer, and your guests will be grumbling along with their stomachs.

❈ Chairs and Tables, Knives and Bowls

Fine-food caterers should be able to provide all the rentals you'll need—dishes, cutlery, glassware, tables and chairs, linens—and they should include it in their quote. Find out the quality of rentals that they'll be using in case you want to upgrade. Restaurant caterers may not provide rentals, so it's best to find out early, and to ask them for referrals if you need to book the rentals yourself. If your non-traditional venue has limited or no kitchen facilities, you also need to find out from your caterer what facilities will be needed—running water, a generator, a cooking truck—and have them included in the contract.

Edith & Kam
The dilemma: How do you sample your wedding meal when you're on a strict pre-wedding diet? Bring Mom!

Most caterers are used to dietary restrictions, but sometimes it's a matter of trust. Organic menus may not be entirely organic and vegetarian meals may not be cooked using separate equipment. Some religious restrictions are harder to cook for than others, and some families are stricter about their diet than others. If your caterer is used to cooking for different needs, you'll be more likely to get what you want. If not, your vegetarian soup could have the odd claw floating in it. Or, at least, it could be made with chicken stock, and any vegetarian worth their *fleur de sel* will taste that immediately. You don't need to alter the menu to fit the needs of a small number of guests—why deny others the chocolate-covered strawberries if only a couple of guests are allergic to them?—but give your caterer plenty of notice for any special meals. If you don't, and your venue doesn't have a kitchen, they won't be able to miraculously produce a wheat-free meal out of their hat.

What to do with all that leftover food? Go green. Ask your caterer if they know of a charity that will accept perishable food donations. Few charities do, because of food safety concerns, but some shelters welcome prepared food in the middle of the night. Otherwise, ask that the leftovers be given to guests and staff.

❧ Raising the Bar

If guests are buying you an expensive gift, says David, the least you can do is buy them a nice dinner. For many people, that includes (read: starts with) alcohol. At the very least, consider a host bar for cocktails and wine with dinner. The lesser of all evils is a cash bar after dinner, but it's always better to throw a smaller party than to charge your guests for attending. If you're in a non-traditional venue, most fine-food caterers are able to provide bar service and a soft bar (mixes, juice, and water), and will let you bring in your own alcohol. **Limiting the bar to a few**

Don't forget the champagne! A limited selection puts a host bar in anyone's price range.

Cutting the Cake

Wedding cake can take many different forms. Cupcakes, cookies, boxes of pre-sliced cake or petit fours, and dessert buffets are alternatives that indulge your sweet tooth without requiring toppling tiers, easily smooshed buttercream frosting, and a prohibitive cake-cutting fee. Get a small cake for the obligatory photo and save it for your midnight snack.

options, provided there is something for everyone, is a great way to make it less expensive. That way, you won't waste money on barely touched liquor that can't be returned. Make your choices intentional, and clearly list them so people aren't confused. For some flair, add a signature cocktail to your list.

Choosing wine can be intimidating, but it should also be fun. If you don't know a lot about wine, the *terroir* is probably not going to be terribly important to you, so don't waste your money hiring a sommelier. If you're worried about embarrassing yourselves, go shopping with the person in your circle of friends who knows the most about wine. Buy a bunch of bottles in your price range, put away the car keys, and have a tasting party. And if you don't know anyone who is knowledgeable about wine, you've probably already skipped this paragraph and ordered the kegs. Keep in mind that staff in large liquor stores can often help you out, and they, or your caterer, can advise you on how much you should buy. Don't be afraid to buy more than you think you'll need, because you can usually return unopened, undamaged bottles for a full refund.

❋ Taking the Cake

Contrary to popular belief—and logic—not everyone loves cake. In this age of health concerns and special dietary needs, many people avoid it. David Connolly says that if cake is all you're serving for dessert, get one that will serve 60% of your guest list; if you're serving other items too, it can be as small as you want. Some couples skip the cake entirely. **Many bakeries rent out fake cakes—Styrofoam forms decorated with icing—for much less than the cost of the real thing.** This is a great option if you want the picture but don't care for cake.

If Styrofoam isn't your favorite flavor, not to worry. The sky's the limit. You're no longer obligated to have fruitcake, carrot cake, or boring old vanilla. That being said, you should probably consider the tastes of your guests—not everyone loves coconut—but that's the beauty of having more than one layer. Cupcakes allow you to have as many flavors as you can dream up. Groom's cakes, long a tradition in the South, are

DAVID CONNOLLY ON HOW NOT TO EAT CAKE: *I beg couples not to smoosh cake in each other's faces, but it still happens. Traditionally, couples cut the cake to represent the first thing they did together. Do you want the first thing you do together to be an act of aggression? Skip the cake-cutting entirely if you like.*

another fun way to add flavor. They're decorated to reflect the groom's interests (topping the list: footballs, golf balls, and laptops) and usually served at the rehearsal dinner. Many couples are now adding them to the dessert table instead, as a way of including an

additional dessert (usually a dark cake) and as a reflection of the groom's involvement. There is a place for that wrestling ring cake after all!

Hear us now: A wedding cake no longer needs to be white. There are endless options for design, as a quick search on the Internet will reveal. The trend is moving toward glamour and glitter, and if that's your thing, dazzle it up to your heart's content. Ideally, the cake should fit your décor. If you want the traditional gigantic white monolith, complete with staircase and fountain, to match your poufy white dress—whether

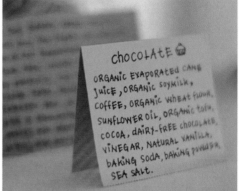

chocolate
ORGANIC EVAPORATED CANE
JUICE, ORGANIC SOYMILK,
COFFEE, ORGANIC WHEAT FLOUR,
SUNFLOWER OIL, ORGANIC tofu,
COCOA, dAiry-FREE chocolate,
VINEGAR, NATURAL VANILLA,
BAKING SODA, BAKING POWDER,
SEA SALT.

it's because of your culture, your taste, or you just love the kitschy appeal—why not? If simple's more your style, you can save a lot of money by buying a slab cake from a bakery and adding floral arrangements or a monogram to unadorned icing.

❋ Your New Best Friend: Finding the Perfect Baker

The best way to find a baker is by word of mouth. Talk to newlyweds, your wedding planner, and other vendors. Take pictures of your ideas to several bakers and see if they're able to re-create them. Sampling is definitely encouraged! When you buy a cake, keep in mind that you're buying more than just flour and sugar. You're also buying delivery and set-up, and an insurance policy that means it will be replaced if something goes wrong. The bigger the bakery, the more insurance you have: more delivery trucks and more back-up cakes. (The woman baking out of her basement is probably not going to have a back-up anything!) Make sure you get a contract, and that it mentions

Sandy & Jason

Sandy and Jason made their yummy vegan cupcakes easier to swallow—for vegetarians and non-vegetarians alike—by making sure the ingredients were no mystery.

when the cake will be delivered, whether someone will assemble it, what the payment schedule is, and what the contingency plan is if something happens to it.

The price range for an average cake is $300 to $500. But beware of cake-cutting fees: Some venues charge anywhere from $1 to $15 per slice to cut a cake brought in from another baker. **If you're going to be charged an exorbitant fee, get a small wedding cake for pictures but serve it at brunch the next day instead.** Have your venue provide the dessert cake and cut it for free, or buy pre-cut cake in boxes to hand out as people leave. Or have cupcakes—no cutting needed! Another thing to keep in mind is that the venue might not let you store your cake in its fridge. Some won't allow you to bring food from elsewhere onto the premises, or there may not be room for it in the kitchen. Other venues allow it, but may charge you for keeping it in their fridge. There's a wide range of policies, so find out well in advance.

Of course, you don't actually have to have cake. It's messy, it's expensive, and few people actually eat it. How about monogrammed cookies, cupcakes, small pastries, or an entire buffet of all of the above? Dessert tables are increasingly popular because they offer alternatives for everyone, not just the cake fiends. Consider having slightly less sinful options like fruit and sorbet as well as the ubiquitous—but blissful—chocolate fountain.

Wedding cakes are part of your décor, which makes picking the design a breeze.

Web Resources Worth Typing For

Wedding planners rely on lots of different resources, and just like you, they often go to the Internet for ideas. From cheapo chatrooms to tango lessons, here are some websites that might inspire you.

1 **TheKnot.com** is one of the biggest wedding websites around. This behemoth covers all things wedding. You can also set up a personal website through The Knot. You have to become a member to access most of the content, but it's free.

2 **WeddingChannel.com** is another mega-wedding website that offers plenty of tools, such as budget calculators and checklists. It will satisfy your fixation for checking things off.

3 **FrugalBride.com** is a great resource for budget-friendly options. It includes the "Babbling Brides Bulletin Board" where brides compare cost-cutting ideas.

4 If you're hiring a DJ, check out the American or Canadian **Disc Jockey Association websites** (www.adja.org / www.cdja.org). Members must be up-to-date on music, equipment, and insurance. You can search for DJs by region and check out the reputations of ones you're interested in.

5 **BridalNetwork.ca** is a North American directory of regional wedding service providers. The listings are broken down into every imaginable category, making it easy to find dove-release companies in St. Catharines or chapels with webcams in Las Vegas.

6 **PrestonBailey.com** is the website of "floral couturier" Preston Bailey. Celebrity weddings abound in his portfolio, so you probably want to pick and choose from his awe-inspiring décor ideas rather than try to emulate Donald Trump's wedding petal-for-petal.

7 Want to know what celebs are wearing on their big days? **InStyleWeddings.com** is the companion site to the giant magazine full of things you can't afford. But the website actually devotes little space to the excesses of celebrity, and more to refreshingly affordable tips and ideas.

8 Don't fear the first dance. Lessons take the pressure off, and are a great escape from planning. **ArthurMurray.com** is a popular chain of dance studios with locations all over the world and specific programs for brides and grooms.

9 **OffbeatBride.com** is the companion site to the book *Offbeat Bride* by blogger Ariel Meadow Stallings. The book is essential reading for couples who hope to stray far, far off the traditional path. The website has tons of ideas for refreshingly different weddings.

10 Of course, some planners have been in business longer than the Internet, and tend to rely on their experience and network of contacts instead. **Your best resource could be a wedding planner.**

Coming Up ROSES

Once upon a time, ordering flowers for your wedding was as easy as going down to the neighborhood florist, opening the FTD book, and picking out whichever predesigned bouquet was in your color. If only it were so simple now. In small towns you may still find florists who offer little choice beyond the giant catalog, but, for better or for worse, you will usually have endless options in the floral department. Say good-bye to the "Sweet Expressions" bouquet (item #06-SW1)... unless you've completely forgotten about the flowers, in which case you can order them online and get them the same day!

Flowers are integral to your wedding because they're so darn romantic. As clichéd as it seems, they're probably the first gift the groom gave the bride, so don't discount their power. But if your budget is limited, they don't need to be excessive. There are three categories of wedding flowers, with varying degrees of necessity: personal, ceremonial, and reception. You can skip the ceremonial flowers, according to Karina, and you can limit reception flowers to centerpieces, but you should have personal flowers.

❧ Be Sure to Wear Some Flowers in Your Hair

Boutonnieres separate the groomsmen from the boys.

Personal flowers include things like bouquets, corsages, and boutonnieres. You can also get petals for the flower girl's basket, garlands if you're getting married on a beach, a toss bouquet if you want to keep your hard-earned bridal bouquet...anything you would wear or carry. Karina believes personal flowers are the most important because they appear in your photos, adding a touch of color to white dresses and black suits, or a stunning contrast to colorful attire. They also give the bridesmaids something to hold, so they don't stand around awkwardly empty-handed (apparently not a problem for groomsmen). Parasols, fans, baskets, and purses are other popular options for the bridesmaids if you want to do something different. You can give corsages and boutonnieres to whomever you'd like (usually your parents), but the groomsmen generally wear boutonnieres so they're not mistaken for some other random guys in dark suits.

Ceremonial flowers are the least important. If you need to cut your flower budget, this is the place to do so. You probably picked a beautiful location for the ceremony, and your guests won't be spending a lot of time there, so why bother? If your ceremony venue looks like it was decorated in the fifties, however, borrow some centerpieces from your reception and place them where they'll be noticed. If you do have the budget for ceremonial flowers, you'll need a lot. Small arrangements will be lost in most churches and temples, so don't be afraid of going too big. Christian weddings often have

Flower Power

You can use flowers to add a dramatic effect without breaking the bank by sticking to one type of flower or using single stems of an exotic flower.

KARINA ON MORE DÉCOR: *Flowers are expensive. You can get a great effect for less with downsized flowers and upgraded linens. Adding colored or textured linens makes a dramatic change. Chair covers look great, but avoid the stretchy, shiny ones and opt for a chair wrap that ties in an elegant bow at the back.*

two large arrangements at the front of the church. Some cultures conduct the ceremony under a canopy, such as a Jewish chuppa or a Hindu mandap, which is frequently decorated with flowers. Flowers can also be hung on the end of pews or on aisle seats, although you can skip this because the only people who will get the great view are you two, and you'll be far too engrossed in your first kiss as a married couple to appreciate it.

Reception flowers usually focus on the table centerpieces, but they can also include elaborate archways, wreaths, and arrangements for things like the cake table, the guestbook table, and even the washrooms. What better way to class up a toilet? However, you and your florist will spend most of your (diminishing) energy on centerpieces. Table centerpieces should capture the colors, theme, or vibe you're going for. You can be creative with shapes and containers, so go nuts. Of course, you don't need to have flowers as a centrepiece at all. Candles or feathers or almost anything can decorate the tables. They shouldn't block people's view of each other, though. If you want tall, dramatic centerpieces, make sure they're slender enough at eye level to see around. How many times have you seen huge, expensive centerpieces immediately relegated to the floor because they were in the way? Once the party's over, consider donating your centerpieces to a seniors' residence. Your guests have already enjoyed them, so why not brighten someone else's morning?

❦ Little Shop of Horrors?

As with everything in weddings, a good place to start looking for a florist is to ask friends and your other vendors for referrals. Ask to see their portfolios, or look at their websites to get a sense of their style and flexibility. Go for a consultation, taking ideas, colors, table size, and numbers with you. Find someone who is compatible with your style, concept, and budget. And don't just give a shopping list of what you want. Given a little free rein, a florist will use what's in season and what looks best to create the look you want. If you absolutely must have gardenias, you'll have to pay an arm and a leg for them, and they'll barely make it through the ceremony. **If you like the look of gardenias but are willing to be flexible, your florist will probably suggest something that will look just as elegant for a much better price, such as peonies in June.**

Reception flowers need not be limited to large, expensive centerpieces. Small arrangements scattered throughout the room look lovely too.

To Have and To Hold

Bridal bouquets come in all shapes and sizes. Gather ideas, but rely on your florist's instincts. She'll know what works best with your gown and with the rest of your flowers. A couple of calla lilies tied with a ribbon may suit your slender gown better than a massive cascade of roses.

Many brides will go to one boutique for a consultation, which takes two or three hours, and get a detailed quote that they can then take to other boutiques to compare prices. As infuriating as this is for the owner of the first boutique, there can be a huge difference in the cost of the same arrangements at different stores, so it is important to shop around. But first you should understand how flowers are priced. They are usually marked

Here's a tip: Hand-tied bouquets are usually less expensive than more structured ones, but are just as beautiful.

up 300% from their wholesale cost because of labor, waste, and unusable flowers (all the flowers in a bride's bouquet have to be perfect). So shop around a bit, but don't nickel and dime a florist who supports your vision. According to Karina, you should plan on spending a minimum of $15 per guest on flowers if you want basic personal, ceremonial, and reception flowers. Expect to spend $20 to $25

KARINA ON FREAKS OF NATURE: *Don't think that you can find flowers to match the bridesmaid's dresses exactly, especially if they're blue. First of all, part of the beauty of flowers is in the subtle variations in color. Any blue flowers you've seen have probably been painted, and they're expensive because of the perception of rarity, the labor that goes into painting them, and the number of flowers that don't survive the painting process.*

per guest for upmarket flowers, and $30 or more per guest for high-end flowers. Most of the floral budget will go to the centerpieces: about $50 to $60 each.

In urban areas, most high-end florists are booked up for the summer a year in advance since many of them only work on one function per date. If you aren't picky about the florist you use, or the florist you like will work on more than one wedding on the same date, you can probably book three to six months before the wedding. Put down the minimum deposit to secure your date, but you might want to keep the deposit in mind when you're picking a florist. Some ask for a 50% non-refundable deposit! That's a lot of money to have tied up in something you can live without.

🌸 Bargain Orchids and Blue Roses

There are a few ways to save money on flowers. One is to set aside your ethical scruples. Flowers from South America or Asia are loads cheaper than those imported from Europe because of lower wages and questionable working conditions. Fair-trade flowers they ain't. But that's where most of our flowers come from (and the source of $19.99/dozen supermarket roses), so you'll be in the majority. If that bothers you, think locally. Visit a green-savvy florist a year ahead of your wedding (if you're that organized!) so you can see what local flowers are available. Local flowers will be cheap without the nasty exploited-labor issue or the burning of massive amounts of airline and diesel fuel.

Time of year is also a consideration when it comes to color. Visit the venue a year in advance, too, so you can see the flowers that are on the grounds. They will probably appear in the background of your wedding photos, so you might want to coordinate your personal flowers with them.

Wendie & Brian
married: 35 years
wedding budget:
$7,000

I knew Wendie was the one for me the first time I laid eyes on her.

I knew Brian was the one because after he asked me out for our first date, I drove by and he was washing the car to take me out. I thought, now there's a nice guy.

🌸 Flower Arranging 101

If you've seen the price of wholesale flowers and decided you can do your own flower arranging, consider this fair warning: There's a reason for that huge mark-up. Your flowers will look wilted, since you probably don't have proper refrigeration for all those centerpieces, and you'll have ruined your manicure in the meantime and spent the day before your wedding working like a slave. Don't even dream of doing it the day of your wedding. Getting

dressed and primped will take longer than you think, and you'll have countless other little things to do that day. Centerpieces are a lot of work: Each one takes about an hour if done properly. Do the math, and it starts to sound pretty scary.

If you're still convinced you can do it, try to make it easy on yourself. Help your flowers make it through the night by using a homemade version of those little packets that come with bouquets: Mix one part Sprite or 7-Up with two parts water and a few drops of bleach. **Stick to one type of flower, which is easier on the budget, or one color, which is easier to arrange.** Orchids are good flowers as they're sturdier than you think and you don't need very many of them for a stunning look. Roses are always a safe bet as they're timeless and easy to arrange. Do not use hydrangeas, a wedding favorite because they come in that most popular of colors, blue. They need lots of water,

Sandy & Jason
Green can be beautiful and economical. Sandy wanted an eco-friendly wedding; Jason wanted it to be affordable. Luckily, Heidi was armed with lots of ideas.

and will die in half an hour without it. Single flowers might be your safest bet.

One dramatic flower, such as a calla lily, in a tall vase on each table, might be sufficient for a small wedding. A rose bowl makes a simple, affordable centerpiece. Another option is to use potted flowers, such as mums, for centerpieces. **To make it really easy on the budget, though, just pick a unique and beautiful venue that needs little adornment.**

Trust your florist to create bouquets that capture
the style and joy of your wedding.

More Petal, Less Metal: Affordable Flowers

Flowers may grow in dirt, but that doesn't mean they're free. Quite the opposite, in fact. But certain flowers are easier to work with and more economical than others.

1 **If you don't have a lot of money to spend on flowers, stick to one type of flower, preferably a white one.** It is always a classic color, is less distracting to the eye, and will look simple rather than cheap.

2 **A rose bowl with a single, floating open white peony is a $6-$10 centerpiece** that will look far more elegant than a $30 centerpiece of cheaper looking mixed flowers.

3 **Roses** are available year-round, and because of low labor costs in South America, they are actually a bargain. **And there are lots of colors to choose from.**

4 **Orchids** also involve low labor prices, meaning they only look expensive. Dendrobium are the least pricey. **Cymbidium are more expensive, but if you use just a couple in a bouquet or arrangement, they add a lot of style for not a lot of money.**

5 **Peonies, when in season (usually about two weeks in June, depending on your location), are a bargain.** If they are out of season and imported from Europe, they are extremely expensive. The good news is they have large heads, so a few can really bulk up a centerpiece.

6 **Hydrangeas are large and can fill out an arrangement, and the Ecuadorian ones are relatively inexpensive.** The really lovely ones you seen in bridal magazines are European or North American. They're bigger and come in a wider range of colors, but are much more expensive.

7 **Tulips, hyacinths, ranunculus, and other spring flowers look sensational in a plain vase.** But do you know how many you will actually need to fill that vase? A basic 6" square vase can easily handle 50 to 60 tulips to get that full look brides love. Tulips run anywhere from $1.00–$4.50/ stem, depending on variety and season. The best time to get them is from January to April.

8 **Calla lilies are available in many varieties, and they're actually not really a lily at all.** The large white imports cost $6-$12/stem, and so do

the lovely little ones that make for gorgeous, compact, hand-tied bouquets. A small bouquet will easily need 30 stems of the small variety to look full.

9 **Local flowers** in season in your area will be cheap. **Visit florists a year ahead of your wedding so you know what will be available locally on your wedding day.**

10 Believe it or not, artificial flowers aren't a cheap option. Well-made silk flowers are very expensive. **Inexpensive fake flowers are obviously fake. Distractingly fake. Horribly fake. Use candles instead!**

SAY CHEESE (Not Cheesy)

Read any number of wedding books, and you'll be told time and again that the only things

that last longer than your wedding day—other than your marriage, one would hope—are

your wedding photos. These pictures will stare at you from your desk or mantel for the rest

of your life. Mere acquaintances will inexplicably ask to see them five years from now. Your

grandchildren will cherish them long after you're gone. So if there's any place on your budget

spreadsheet where you shouldn't cut corners, says Heidi, it's here. Don't trust your priceless

memories to just any weekend warrior with a digital camera and Photoshop®.

❋ Sears Pose or *Cinema Vérité*?

There are two styles of wedding photography: formal and photojournalistic. Formal photos are blatantly posed shots; photojournalistic photos are candid and impromptu. There are advantages and disadvantages to both. In formal photos, the photographer will make sure that everyone who should be there is included and that everyone looks their best, but the resulting photos will be unnatural and, well, quite possibly boring. Just look at your parents' wedding pictures, with the wedding party lined up neatly on either side of the wide-eyed couple, and you'll get the idea.

Jean & Tom
married: 56 years
wedding budget:
$500

If given the opportunity to do it again I would do it exactly the same way.

It was simple . . . beautiful . . . the beginning of our life together. I would do it the same way also.

Photojournalism captures the energy and emotion of your wedding in a way that formal photos can't, but it often involves unflattering postures and may not include some important people. Some people assume photojournalism is easier and that they can get just anyone to take candid shots. On the contrary, it takes a lot of skill to get crisp candid photos with perfect lighting and still manage to avoid cutting off heads. More and more, photographers are blending the two styles so that you will end up with some formal posed shots and lots of candid pictures. Decide how much of each style you would prefer, and find a photographer who is willing and able to do that for you.

You also need to think about whether you want digital or film. Most photographers now work with digital because of the advantages. They can take a lot more pictures; prints are cheaper and can be easily incorporated into professional albums or

Candid shots record the
authentic moments
in between formal poses.

video montages; the couple can decide afterward which ones they would like in black and white, so the photographer won't have to carry two cameras; and the couple gets a CD of the proofs so they can print them whenever they want. However, some photographers still work in film because of the perception that it's more professional, because the couple receives physical proofs, and because negatives will last longer than a disk. Have some idea of what you might like before talking to photographers.

❀ A Picture's Worth a Thousand Bucks

Professional photographers come in full-time and part-time flavors. Obviously, full-time photographers should be the most skilled. **But part-time photographers may give you great quality at a cheaper price if they've had professional training and spend their weekends working weddings out of love as much as out of fiscal necessity.** Full-time professionals charge around $2,000 to $5,000, depending on the package; part-time photographers often charge slightly less, although you may have to shop around to find one who does.

Even with all these decisions made, it will still be hard to pick a photographer. Start early, advises Heidi, since the better ones may be booked a year in advance. No matter where you live, there are hundreds of photographers, and all of their proof books look great. To find one who won't disappoint you, talk to friends whose photos you like, and ask your other vendors, as they'll know photographers' reputations. Photographers probably won't be able to give you references from other clients, but they may be able to give you references from vendors they've worked with. Also, check whether they

Give your photographer a list of the formal photos you want so he can plan ahead.

have a busy schedule: If you're interviewing in June and they're able to meet you on a Saturday, you know there's something wrong.

✿ Becoming an Art Critic

Look critically at each photographer's work. They have to work fast to get every photo you want, and every one has to be perfect. So don't look just at their portfolios. They've cherry-picked the best pictures from a bunch of weddings, so of course the pictures are going to look great. Heidi recommends that you ask to see a proof book or contact sheet

> **HEIDI ON MAKING THE MOST OF YOUR PHOTOS:** *Everyone puts so much thought into the wedding album—they spend all this money ($1,000+), have it out for one year, then put it away. You get all the images in the proof book, so you have your album right there. Instead, I suggest hanging a beautiful photograph, framed and matted, up on your wall, where you can see it and cherish it every day.*

so that you can see every photo taken at a wedding, from beginning to end. Also look at photos from different weddings to make sure they're slightly different and not all the same cookie-cutter style.

Make sure your photographer is flexible with packages. Most photographers have packages that cost different amounts depending on the number of hours you would like them at the wedding and the number of prints and albums. Find out if yours is able to adjust the packages to suit you. Make sure he'll be bringing a back-up camera and an

If you're comfortable with your photographer, it will show in your photos. If his attempts to coax a smile make you cringe instead, think twice about hiring him.

assistant to help wrangle guests. And make sure he has a back-up photographer, should anything disastrous happen to him at the last minute.

Don't be surprised if a large studio doesn't allow you to meet with your specific photographer before the contract is signed, or even before the wedding day. The studio is just scared that you may hire the photographer independently at a lower price. If the studio won't let you meet your photographer, try elsewhere. It's not enough to see a portfolio; you need to know if you have chemistry with the photographer, too. Wedding photos capture emotional moments, so if you're not comfortable with your photographer, your pictures are going to reflect that discomfort. They won't look as good as they could look, no matter who your photographer is.

When you get your contract, read it carefully to make sure there are no surprises and that the details you've arranged are correct. Here's Heidi's list of must-check contract points:

- ❀ the number of hours the photographer will take pictures
- ❀ the number of rolls of film or images you will receive
- ❀ the number of albums and prints you will receive (or the length of the wedding video)
- ❀ the number of pictures that will be in color and in black and white
- ❀ whether or not the photographer will have an assistant and a back-up photographer
- ❀ whether or not the photographer will charge you for travel
- ❀ the total cost of the package and the payment schedule
- ❀ the cancellation policy

Ligia & Tony

Ligia paid careful attention to every detail, despite Tony's laid-back attitude to the wedding, and the reward was fabulous photos that perfectly capture the couple's spirit.

❀ Practice Makes Perfect

Speaking of that cancellation policy, engagement photos are a great way to test-drive your photographer, if your budget allows. If his or her personality during the shoot makes you cringe rather than glow, or you're unimpressed by the finished product, you still have time to find another photographer. As a bonus, you get professional photos of both of you in something other than formal wear, and you'll get used to the whole bizarre experience of being followed around by your own paparazzi. By the time your wedding day hits, you'll automatically strike your most fabulous pose every time you see a camera.

If you've seen engagement photos of earnest couples clad in sweaters and jeans, crouching in the autumn leaves with their golden retriever, and had to stifle your laugh-

> **HEIDI ON PERSONALITY PLUS:** *When interviewing photographers, consider their personality. It's high school all over again! You're not looking for an introverted artiste. Your photographer needs to interact with your guests and get them moving, and it needs to be fun. But he or she can't be so outgoing as to intrude in every situation; a photographer should be able to become almost invisible in order to get great candid shots.*

ter, it may not seem like your kind of thing, but the pay-off will be amazing wedding pictures. **Many photographers include engagement photos in their packages, which may put the cost within your reach.** Worst-case scenario: You'll learn—the hard way—to tilt your chin up and practice your smile.

To get tons of fun pictures your photographer might miss, place disposable cameras at each table.

To save your photographer from any nasty surprises, check with your ceremony venue for its policy on photographers. Many have restrictions on where photographers and videographers can be during different parts of the ceremony, or if they can be there at all. If your photographer is not familiar with your venues, try to arrange for him to visit the sites before your wedding so he can plan ahead. Give him a schedule of the wedding day—so he knows where to be and when—and a list of the formal photographs you'd like taken as well as the people and places you hope will be captured in candid shots. Designate a family member to help point out the people and places. And make sure to tell your family to show up for formal photos. Grandma may not assume you want to include her, as obvious as it might seem to you.

✿ Video Killed the Budget

Many of the *Rich Bride Poor Bride* planners suggest that if you need to cut costs, eliminate the wedding video. If you go to bridal shows, you'll be confronted with a long line of booths blasting professional videos worthy of MTV. And they can cost about as much as a music video. **If you're tight for cash or you just know you're not going to bother watching it after your first anniversary (if even then), skip the video entirely.**

However, wedding videos do have their place. You can't be everywhere on your wedding day, after all. And if many of your family members can't make the wedding because of distance, it's a great opportunity to share your day with them, says Heidi. If you decide on a wedding video, keep your expectations realistic. You will not get a Hollywood production with perfect lighting and sound. But you should get an accurate reflection of the spirit of your day. A lot of the rules that apply to your search for a photographer also apply to looking for a videographer. Look for one who produces

A wedding video will mean the world to family far away.

the style of video you want, and who has a reputation for being reliable and unobtrusive. Ask how involved you can be in the editing process, and if you can get the full-length version as well as the edited copy. **If a videographer is out of the question but you would like a video record of the big moments, borrow a friend's camcorder and set it up on a tripod for the ceremony and speeches.** Just don't expect an Oscar for your cinematography. For a more public wedding video, come get married on *Rich Bride Poor Bride*.

Making the Most of Wedding Shows

Wedding shows can be overwhelming, but with these suggestions from Heidi in hand, you can make the most of your show experience.

1 Bride-to-be, do not go by yourself! **Bring your groom, your mother, or a bridal party member.** Beware of bringing too many people. A suggested maximum is three people in total (including the bride). This way nobody will get lost in the crowd.

2 **Be sure to print mailing labels with the following information**: name, address, phone number, email address, wedding date. You will find that many vendors have drawings for door prizes, and this will save you from writing all your information at every vendor's booth.

3 **Bring a notebook and pen and USE IT!** You will never remember which vendor told you what, so you will need to take notes.

4 If you really hate receiving spam, but want to get as much information as you can and participate in the drawings and giveaways, register in advance for an email address from one of the many free services like Hotmail or Yahoo. When filling out contest entry forms and inquiry sheets, use this address. **When the wedding is over you can simply cancel the account and avoid any further wedding-related emails.**

5 **Bring swatches of material or ribbons with your wedding colors on them.** This will help bakers, decorators, and florists make appropriate suggestions as to what they can do for you.

6 Beware of vendors who will only offer show discounts on the day of the show. If you do not have the opportunity to talk with them in-depth, how do you know they are right for you? **Ask vendors if they will guarantee the "show price" if you are willing to book an appointment with them for the following week.**

7 Do not get discouraged! **If you are at the show to get new ideas and you do not see anything, ask a professional in that area of expertise.** They have plenty of photos and ideas if you take the time to talk to them and explain your wedding theme or vision.

8 **Do not waste your time talking about services that you have already booked.** Also, if you run into your vendors, be sure to say hi but do not discuss details with them. They will not remember afterward that you asked to change your first dance song or the wedding album cover.

9 **Attend the fashion show.** Each show will detail the latest gown styles, colors, and fashionable accessories available for that year. It will greatly assist you in your search for that perfect gown.

10 **Check out the limos, even if you have no intention of renting one.** They're the perfect place to relax and re-group when you need a time-out from the show.

All About HAR-MONEY

Weddings are remembered for the music. The little girl dancing on her father's feet, your

grandmothers doing the actions to "YMCA" together, the conga line that has your best man

grabbing your aunt—these are the things that make a wedding memorable. If you don't pay

enough attention to it, or you don't consider your guests' tastes when you choose the music,

it could be memorable for all the wrong reasons.

When you sit down to plan music, Heidi suggests you think of it as a distinct aspect of

your wedding. For example, don't plan ceremony music when you're planning the ceremony;

plan music for the whole day and determine how it will fit in to your ceremony. The most impressive thing she's seen (well, heard) was a wedding in which the music for the entire day—from the ceremony to cocktails to dinner to the dance—was consistent. The couple decided what kind of music would best reflect them, and then had the same style played all day. Even though the ceremony, dinner, and dance musicians were hired separately, the result was cohesive and the transitions were flawless. Naturally you'll

> **HEIDI ON AVOIDING *AMERICAN IDOL*:** *Having friends sing during the wedding can add something special to your ceremony without costing anything. But if you know they're not up to it, quickly find another option rather than put your guests through an awkward performance.*
>
> *Find another way for your friends to participate in the ceremony.*

have to mix up the dance music a bit, but you can probably intersperse enough of your chosen style of music to give the impression of consistency. If your style is jazz, slow dances can be songs by Harry Connick, Jr. or Michael Bublé. Of course, if your style is rock, you'll have similar problems with the ceremony music, but at least you'll have fun trying to convince the organist to add The White Stripes to his or her repertoire.

❀ Beyond "Here Comes the Bride"

When planning ceremony music, it's common to have:

- ❀ background music for about half an hour before the ceremony as guests arrive
- ❀ music for the bridesmaids as they walk up the aisle

* processional music for the bride (which could be a continuation of the bridesmaids' music)

* a song for the signing of the marriage license

* recessional music for when you walk back down the aisle together

Ceremony music will often be dictated by the venue. A place of worship might tell you what songs you can and can't have during the ceremony. For instance, Wagner's "Wedding March" is usually avoided in synagogues because of the composer's well-known anti-Semitism. Many churches will limit ceremonial music to hymns, so pick one

Your venue may limit your processional music. But your recessional music can often be anything you want, so feel free to break out the Bee Gees.

Cinzia & David

Cinzia took time to enjoy the music at her gothic-inspired wedding, from her dance with her father to a special performance by her new brother-in-law.

that has some meaning for both of you. Some places of worship are flexible and will let you have contemporary music, or will allow it if you're getting married outdoors. Most are pretty lenient when it comes to the recessional, though, so once the ceremony is over, you're probably free to walk (or shadow box) out to the theme from Rocky. Just check with your officiant first.

When I saw your father walking down the aisle, I thought: Smashing, boy, this is going to be great!

My father?!

You should also check whether or not the venue will let just anyone touch the organ or piano. **Churches are very protective of their instruments and may only allow certain musicians to play them. The upside of this restriction is that they often charge very little — usually $50 to $100 — to hire their organist.** But ceremony music can run the gamut from basic to extravagant. On the other end of the spectrum, you can pay up to $5,000 for an opera singer or a string quartet. Somewhere in the middle you might consider solo instrumentalists, such as an acoustic guitarist, a violinist, or whatever you think is appropriate for your ceremony.

✾ Music to Dine By

It's really important to have background music during the cocktail hour. Especially when guests are starting to trickle in at the beginning, music lets them know they're in the right place and makes those awkward silences slightly more tolerable. Cocktail music doesn't have to be elaborate. If you've hired musicians for the ceremony, they may be willing to stick around and perform during the cocktail hour for a small additional fee. Or your DJ might build it into your package. If your venue is a hotel or country club, they probably pipe music into the lobby, so ask them if you can pick the type of music. Most subscribe to a satellite service, so you may be able to pick an appropriate channel. If there is a piano in the lobby, they probably also have a list of pianists they can recommend who are familiar with the piano, so be sure to ask.

Dinner music can follow the same formula: Either pay the ceremony musicians to stick around a bit longer, or have your DJ do the background music. However, more and more couples are hiring strolling musicians to provide entertainment during the meal. An accordion, a guitar, even a violin—it's a great way to take your wedding to the next level.

❧ A Little Night Music

The reception music is one of those things that everyone will talk about. Depending on your budget, you can hire a DJ or a band, or even both. **DJs charge anywhere from $500 to $5,000, depending on how much you want them to do, and expect to pay around $2,500 for a band.** Book your musicians at least six months in advance. The best way to find out about DJs and bands is through referrals. Ask your other vendors, specifically the venue. They'll be able to tell you what DJs are booked there time and again, which is a good indication that they're first-rate.

Cinzia & David
David's brother shares his love of music, so he wrote the couple a song, earning a standing ovation.

You'll see lots of DJs and musicians at wedding shows, which is a great way to find out who's out there, but don't book anyone at the show. Arrange private appointments to meet with any that interest you, then follow up with the Better Business Bureau.

> **HEIDI ON SLICK SLIDESHOWS:** *Slideshows are a fun, poignant feature, but you've got enough on your plate. If you want control over it but can't do it yourself, hire a professional. Some videographers create a photo montage, capture some of the day, and add the footage to the end before it's shown. But that's expensive. For a smaller fee, many DJs include a standard slideshow in their package.*

Your first dance is your chance to spend quality time together, so make it count.

People love to complain about bad DJs, so if there's any dirt out there, you can usually find it. When picking a DJ, keep in mind the taste of your guests as well as the tastes of both of you. Much like a used car salesman, a certain breed of DJ will set off your corny meter. Lots of people love these guys, and they're hugely successful, but if you're worried they'll make your guests (or you) feel uncomfortable, go elsewhere. Heidi was at a wedding where the DJ had the guests hold a long balloon between their legs and pass it to each other. The families were very religious and were horrified. So be sure to ask your DJ what games they might play, and warn them ahead of time if the games risk offending your guests.

❀ Ixnay on "YMCA"

Many DJs list their services on their website. You may also be able to look at their song list online. Even if you can't, you should be able to pick some songs in advance, like your first dance, the dance with your parents, and the wedding party's dance. You should also tell them your favorite songs, what styles of music your guests will like, and anything you absolutely do not want played. Give them lots of input (or go elsewhere if they don't let you), but you don't have to pick every song—a good DJ will get a sense of what he should play from a list of your likes and dislikes and what your guests might like. If you're not really sure what older family members might like, ask your parents for ideas. Ask your wedding party for their favorite songs as well. They'll appreciate being able to put their mark on the day and pick songs that reflect your friendship. You don't need to ask the rest of your guests for their favorite songs; they're expecting the work to be done for them. If they want a specific song, they'll request it from the DJ. Whatever you do, do not pick offensive songs, even if it's your absolute favorite song. There's a time and place for 50 Cent. Anything involving your grandparents is not it.

A good DJ will be courteous to your guests when it comes to requests. Heidi always asks DJs to respond positively to requests from your "do not play" list. Your guest will feel like an idiot if the DJ says the bride and groom specifically requested that "Celebration" not be played. Instead, he could say something like, "I've got lots of requests, so I'll do what I can!" Most people will eventually forget that they even requested a song, but if they don't, don't expect the DJ to deal with angry guests. That's a situation where a wedding planner becomes indispensable.

First dances don't have to be intimidating. Ballroom dance lessons will make it a breeze, not to mention give you a welcome diversion from wedding planning—and a chance to steal the show from your nimble-footed aunts and uncles.

❋ The Wedding Band

Bands are great because they add a lot of energy and are usually pretty impressive, but they won't provide all the services that a DJ will. Wedding bands are pretty versatile and might take requests, but bar bands may not be able to play music that will make your 80-year-old grandpa happy. Keep that in mind when you're picking a band—your favorite band may be great in a bar full of people with similar taste, but that doesn't necessarily translate to a wedding. Ask if the band has wedding experience and whether it's able to play a range of styles.

Many couples will hire a DJ as well as a band so that when the band takes breaks, the DJ takes over and plays the music the band can't, such as polkas, the chicken dance, the Macarena… Of course, this is going to cost you a little more, but the DJ can probably do ceremony and cocktail music too. Whatever you do, make sure you can see the band in action. If they play in bars, go to see them there; otherwise, get some kind of audition. If you can't see them, don't hire them.

❋ Prepare for the Parade of Bad Hair

DJs are technical wizards, so they're often the best person to run the infamous slideshow. The slideshow is typically made up of pictures of the bride and groom as they grow up, and then pictures of them together. Often members of the wedding party or family will put a slideshow together, which is the cheapest option, especially if you have a friend with the right skills and computer software to do it. However, it should be a toast to the couple, not a roast, so if you're at all worried about what might show up, insist on seeing it first. One way to control the slideshow is to do it yourself, if either of you actually has the time and the ability, or hire a DJ or videographer to do it if you

want it to be spectacular. A slideshow can kill your wedding reception if it's too long, so keep it at about seven to ten minutes, and put it to music to keep the energy going.

❊ More than Music

In addition to running your slideshow, DJs can add a lot of interaction and entertainment to your event beyond the music. Typically they'll have games, and they can bring in a light show, dry ice, and fireworks, depending on what you're willing to pay them. Heidi stresses that it's a great idea to add entertainment to your reception beyond dancing because entertaining your guests throughout the day really shows them you care about them. But that entertainment shouldn't be the same old thing. Enough with the dry ice already: Try to add things that are original and are special to the two of you, and within your budget. Heidi's seen flamenco dancers, opera singers, and acrobats, but some of these options are really expensive. Be creative and you can probably come up with ideas that are affordable. A couple that loved rap music and break dancing hired three dancers to perform at their wedding. The performance was incredible, and the guests were thrilled, especially since it was something that really reflected the couple.

Strike up the Band

DJs can do just about anything, but a band is really special. Having musicians perform throughout the day will keep your guests entertained and impressed.

Folk dancers get the crowd wound up—and often very involved—and incorporate your cultural heritage in a way that adds energy to your reception and something memorable for guests who come from a different background.

Doing your own music may be affordable, but Heidi says it's not an option. Whether you burn a bunch of CDs or load up the iPod, you're just asking for trouble. There will be problems with the sound level changing, or the CD skipping, and you or your wedding party shouldn't have to spend half the night searching for a request. **If your budget is limited, just get the most basic DJ package.** It might cost you $500, but this is the biggest party you'll ever throw, so get a professional to take care of the music.

Scared that picture of you in your headgear might surface in your slideshow? Hire a professional and control the content.

Vendors are an indispensable part of every wedding. But dealing with vendors can be intimidating for the uninitiated. Find your courage with the tips below.

1 **Relax and let the pros handle the heavy lifting.** Catering, flowers, music, etc., should be done by someone you are paying. Unless your cousin is a gifted floral designer and has offered to do the flowers, they are not going to turn out like the picture you gave him from a magazine.

2 Choose your vendors based on referrals. **Talk to family, friends, other vendors, your wedding planner—anyone that's been to an event recently.** Ask them about the food, the service, the entertainment, and whatever else you're looking for, then find out who the vendors were.

3 Be skeptical of certain referrals, but don't rule them out. Some vendors get a commission for recommending others. **However, if you know that a vendor has an exceptional reputation, chances are that anyone he recommends will also be first-rate.** He probably won't risk his own reputation by recommending sub-par vendors.

4 **Book service providers and venues early to ensure you get exactly what you want.** This also gives you plenty of time to look at other options if your first choice does not work out.

5 Know your vendors. **The reputation of the vendors you choose is very important.** Selecting ones with impeccable workmanship will help minimize all unpleasant surprises on the day of the wedding.

6 Keep your options open. If you feel that you need to hire a specific vendor, you won't be the one in the driver's seat. **To negotiate effectively, you must be able to walk away.**

7 Negotiate, but not necessarily for the best price. **Many vendors are willing to throw in extras and provide better service rather than lower their fee.** Convince your DJ to come an hour early and do the music during cocktails, for example. It'll help him get your business, and it's not a lot of extra work.

8 **Get it in writing.** When booking vendors, make sure everything that's discussed, such as special deals and arrangements that you would like to be included in the package for the quoted price, is written in the contract.

9 **Follow up with all vendors to confirm arrangements two months before the wedding date.**

10 Make sure you thank them. **If they've done a great job, send them a thank you note to let them know you appreciate their contribution to your day.**

GIFTS *for* YOU, GIFTS *for* THEM

So you're getting married for the presents. Hey, who isn't? Or maybe you've been living together for ten years and all you really need is the vacation of your dreams. Welcome to the world of gift registries.

Believe it or not, wedding gifts are a relatively recent invention. Hard to imagine in the age of six-figure weddings, but once upon a time—less than a century ago, actually—weddings were far more low-key than the current crop of pseudo-Broadway production numbers. There were no stretch Hummers. There were no $60 centerpieces. There were no seven-course dinners or 400-person guest lists. And there used to be little expectation of a gift. Indeed, all that was required was the presence of family and close friends to mark the joyous occasion. Even more unbelievable, the guests actually expected gifts from the couple.

⚙ Shop 'Til You Drop

As you wander the aisles of a giant store with your bar-code scanner and wish list in hand, you're bound to feel guilty about the materialism of it all. Don't worry, says Heidi.

> **ANGELIQUE ON REMEMBERING EACH OTHER:** *While your minds are on all these gifts, don't forget each other. It's nice to find out that during all the craziness of planning, you each took time to think about the person making it all possible. Think of things that will help make marriage as special as the wedding, such as gift cards for spa days, concerts, and dinners.*

You're actually doing your guests a favor. Although technically you're not supposed to ask for gifts, and traditionally guests aren't obligated to give them, etiquette dictates that they at least repay you for the dinner in one form or another. You're just making it easier for them to do so. Not to mention the fact that you'll be grateful for every gift you get. **Just remember, not registering means multiple coffeemakers — and not nearly enough gift receipts.**

You can also take solace in the fact that filling a registry is hard work. At first it sounds like fun — you get to spend the day shopping together for everything you could possibly want, and you don't have to spend a thing! Until you're staring at a wall of toasters, arguing over the merits of wide slots versus retro design, and wondering what your friends will think of you for asking for a $200 toaster.

It's harder than it sounds. So make a list of what you need before you go. Research what brands are best. Know how you want to decorate. Department stores are often

We're getting presents! After toiling through the tiresome registry process, you'll have earned every gift.

helpful—they'll have advisers who can instruct you in the foreign language of place settings and bar ware, suggest items you might never have thought of, provide sample lists you can adapt to your needs, and calculate how many gifts you should register for. Start registering shortly after you get engaged in case anyone feels a strong desire to buy you lucky kids an engagement gift. You don't need to register for everything at once; just pick a few small things and do the rest by the time your shower invitations are sent. Check if anything you're registering for early may be discontinued by your wedding day, so you don't have your heart broken when that state-of-the-art VCR doesn't show up on the gift table.

⚙ Playstations, Fishing Boats, and Other Necessities

By the way, it's okay to add a big-ticket item or two. Often this is a signal to the wedding party that they should chip in on one big gift. **And many stores have a completion program that allows you to buy anything left on your registry at a discount, usually for up to one year after your wedding.** The perfect chance to get that flat-panel television you so desperately need! Your parents may also be looking for suggestions on large gifts. Heidi once attended a shower where an entire suite of stainless steel appliances, a gift from the bride's parents, was wheeled in, item by item, for all to see. All that was missing was an appearance by Bob Barker. Over-the-top, yes, but not necessarily uncharacteristic—she also knows couples who have received homes or luxury cars from doting parents.

It's important to pick things in a wide range of prices, and to pick a lot. Your guests will feel mildly irritated by a list with only a dozen items on it, despite your attempts to impress them with your restraint. Give them lots of choice so they can pick something they can afford and feel happy giving you. And it's okay to have more than one registry.

Gifts Galore

Nothing brings out the generosity in people like a wedding. Everyone gets gifts: your attendants, your guests, and perhaps even your parents. And, of course, the two of you. Just don't forget to buy gifts for each other. Your soon-to-be spouse deserves a little something to go with the ring.

Many couples register at a department store for the basics—linens, pots and pans, toilet brushes—and at one or two specialty shops as well. Gift boutiques and china shops allow you to choose nonessentials, like vases, picture frames, martini shakers, and the all-important china pattern, if that's your thing. You can even register at unlikely places such as hardware stores. Go ahead, register for that chainsaw! When someone inevitably asks what they can get you that "isn't boring," you'll have a great answer.

At least one of your registries should be online so that out-of-town guests can buy off your registry and have the gifts delivered to you. Most chain stores are equipped for this, so no worries there. But what if you already have everything you need?

You're on the threshold of a new life. If your old life is fully stocked, just ask for cash.

◉ Cash Cash Cash

Yes, you can ask for cash instead. But be sure you're ready to explain why. People want to know that their money isn't just going to pay for the wedding itself. **If you're saving for a house or a hot tub, and you furnished your apartment long ago, guests will usually be happy to help you out with a cash gift.** Whatever you do, says Heidi, do not have a money tree. Money trees are those real or fake or crafty trees that you drape or clip cash on. Never mind that a wedding crasher might walk out with it; it's offensive, and very embarrassing for guests who brought gifts. A solid box with a slot for cards will do the trick with much more subtlety.

Another option is a honeymoon registry, offered by many travel agents, resorts, and cruise lines. If all you want is your dream vacation, but need a little help to make it happen, guests can buy stuff for you like a room upgrade, spa services, excursions, casino chips, or dinner at a nice restaurant, or they can contribute to the cost of your plane tickets.

✺ Gifts? What Gifts?

Of course, once you've gone through the process of registering, or know that all you really need is money, you can't actually ask anyone for gifts. How presumptuous! Instead of printing it on your invitations—a huge faux pas—tell your parents and your wedding party your wishes. Most guests will know to ask them anyway. Make sure the members of your entourage are well-informed so they don't direct people to the wrong store, and so they can tell people the web addresses of your online registries.

It is okay, however, to mention your registries or preference for cash on your "wedsite," says Heidi. If you've set up a website for your wedding, guests will naturally expect to find all relevant information there. To feign subtlety, set up a "Frequently Asked Questions" page. Under the question, "Where are you registered?" list the stores you're registered at, add links to your online registries, indicate how checks should be made out, or just say, "We have everything we need except a house to put it in, so we would appreciate it if you contributed to our down payment fund instead."

Cathy & Randy
married: 25 years
wedding budget:
$5,000

It seems that if you hold your wedding in a more expensive place, people feel obligated to bring more expensive gifts. We were at a corn roast on the beach and people got us Tupperware.

I can't comment on that...Yeah, it was your family.

Once you've opened the gifts, the work isn't over. Okay, opening the gifts isn't exactly work, but it'll feel like it to those who are forced to watch you. If you're throwing a brunch the morning after the wedding, give people an opportunity to hit the road before the gift-opening starts, or at least warn them about it in advance. Keep careful track of who gave you what so that you're ahead of the game when it comes time to send thank you notes.

If you receive gift cards, be sure to check if they have expiration dates or maintenance fees. Your guests spent all that money for your benefit, not the store's shareholders'. You'll also save yourself a lot of grief by telling your entourage how checks should be made out. If the bride's not changing her name, she may not be able to cash

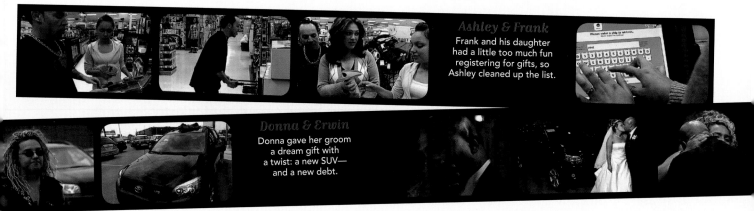

Ashley & Frank
Frank and his daughter had a little too much fun registering for gifts, so Ashley cleaned up the list.

Donna & Erwin
Donna gave her groom a dream gift with a twist: a new SUV— and a new debt.

checks made out to some mythical person the groom's grandma wishes existed. In fact, even if you are changing your name, it's still a good idea to request checks in your maiden name. Many banks require a copy of your marriage certificate and driver's license in your new name in order to change your account, and that means waiting for months for the government to process them.

Spoil your guests with multiple favors. Buying in bulk on the Internet makes it possible even on a budget.

☼ Thanks for Coming, and Here's Your Espresso Machine

As mentioned earlier, there was a time when guests expected gifts from the bride and groom, rather than the other way around. The couple was supposed to show their gratitude to guests for showing up to eat all their food, drink too much mead, and hit on the bridesmaids. In the name of compromise, however, now everyone gets a gift, and the world of favors has become a minefield of expectations, competition, and, inevitably, inflated expenditures.

Because of the traditional roots of favors, they began as homemade gifts—wine, jam, candy—and to some extent these traditions persist. European weddings still feature almonds coated in sugar, meant to signify good luck and fertility. Rarely are these the only favors any more, though. As weddings became showier in the last century, the favor became the crystal dish that held the candies, then instead of a useless tchotchke, an espresso cup and saucer, and then as the impracticality of one espresso cup became obvious, a whole set.

They stuck by you when you asked them to lick 200 stamps and called to gripe about your in-laws. Your attendants deserve something special, don't they?

◈ Wedding Party Loot

There's no rule on what to spend on wedding party gifts, but $50–$75 each is a good start. Angelique suggests making each gift personal, but sometimes it's easier to have a uniform gift for all.

Other weddings feature multiple favors, such as one that Angelique planned. Guests caught waiting in the sun for the ceremony to start were offered bottles of water

> **ANGELIQUE ON WEDDING PARTY LOOT:** *There's no rule on what to spend on wedding party gifts, but $50 each is a good start. I suggest personal gifts, but uniform gifts are easier. I'm tired of jewelry, flasks, money clips, and business card holders. But I love sports equipment, handbags, cologne and perfume, movie or concert tickets, and gift cards.*

with personalized labels. They received fans to cool them as they continued to roast in the sun or became verklempt. When they danced too much, they were given slippers to soothe their feet, and sample bottles of cologne or perfume for when all that sun and dancing turned them a little, er, ripe.

Believe it or not, such a suite of practical favors can actually be affordable. The Internet is naturally the place to start, and even the cologne and perfume can be bought in bulk direct from the manufacturer to save money. It's

Liquid Love: regardless of Angelique's warnings, the flask remains a popular gift for groomsmen. Try making it more personal with etchings or engravings.

easy to go overboard in the favors category—Angelique knows of one bride who gave out $75 hand-carved sculptures of the Horseshoe Falls to all of her guests—but it's equally easy to make cuts in this area if you're over budget. You can spend as little as $5 per person, plus a dollar or two for wrapping, as long as you think of things that people will appreciate. Environmental-minded gifts, such as bulbs or tree seedlings, are popular, but you might want to have back-up favors for guests whose trees won't survive an overseas flight.

Gourmet treats are budget-friendly favors that won't gather dust.

☸ Our Gift to You Is World Peace

If the thought of wasting money on something that's just going to end up at the next yard sale makes you cringe, consider donating the cost of favors—at least $5 per guest—instead. In lieu of a favor, announce that a donation has been made on the guests' behalf to a charity that has some meaning to both of you. It's a thoughtful way to incorporate something you care about into your day, with the added bonus of not unwittingly going over budget—and not having to wrap 200 favors.

The old tradition of handmade or food gifts can still work. Mixed CDs are becoming popular, and pretty much guarantee that the groom will want to help out. Local specialties, such as maple syrup or ice wine, are often appreciated if many of your guests have come from far away. If your aunt's fudge is to die for, give a couple of pieces to each guest with a copy of her recipe. Candy is usually a pretty safe bet: **If you're short on funds, a small box of truffles is elegant and economical.** No favor is wrong in the right context, however. One of Angelique's couples gave out mini-vibrators at their goth wedding, and everyone went home happy.

Minding your Matrimonial Ps and Qs

It may seem old-fashioned, but etiquette makes everything run smoothly. Here are our proper etiquette tips that will help you act rationally when emotions run high and avoid embarrassing social blunders on your special day.

1 Under no circumstances should you mention your registry—or worse yet, that you'd prefer cash—in your invitation. Tell your wedding party and let them spread the word.

2 Be nice to your vendors, and they'll go out of their way to do their best for you. Be rude to them, and you'll get exactly what you paid for—if that. Make sure you send them thank you notes after the wedding to show how much you appreciated their contribution.

3 Be nice to your bridal party. They're spending a lot of money and time to help you out, so have some consideration for their time and don't make any unreasonable demands. Unless they're being unreasonable. **If you're stuck planning your own bachelor party, it may be time to reconsider your choices.**

4 Seek help from friends and family by asking them for help. They'd probably be thrilled to help, but if you just assign work to them and expect it to get done, they may resent the imposition and not do it well. **All you have to do is ask.**

5 If you haven't received responses from guests by the RSVP date, it is perfectly fine to call them to confirm their attendance. Out of a hundred or more reply cards, a couple are bound to get lost in the mail.

6 Include instructions from the ceremony venue in your program. **It's okay to include a tasteful note asking guests to turn off their cellphones and refrain from taking pictures during the ceremony.**

7 Send thank you cards to everyone. **If they didn't give you a gift, thank them for attending.** You're not supposed to ask for gifts, so they're not obligated to give you one.

8 Don't mass-produce your thank you cards. **Write a personal note in each one, mentioning the gift they gave you or how you intend to spend the cash.** And both of you must sign it.

9 **"Thanks for the bounced check!"** If a check you receive as a gift bounces, phone the guest and explain the problem. If they don't send a replacement check, don't bother calling them again. And in this case, it's okay not to send them a thank you card.

10 **Don't re-gift—it could come back to haunt you.** If you do receive a duplicate of something but weren't given gift receipts, mention the problem to the gift-giver you're closest to and ask their permission to give it to a friend or family member who could really use it.

Start with a Kiss: THE CEREMONY

It goes without saying that your ceremony is the most important part of your wedding day.

Or does it? You'd never know it from the amount of attention and money thrown at every

other element of most weddings. But without the ceremony, it's just an expensive party.

The part where you pledge your lifelong love and faithfulness to one person forever and ever

probably deserves equal billing.

If you don't consider marriage a religious commitment, you probably don't need a

priest. Non-religious or civil ceremonies (when not performed by Elvis) can be performed by a public official or a humanist officiant, depending on where you live. You might have a hard time envisioning an appropriate non-religious ceremony if all that springs to mind is a five-minute exercise in bureaucracy in front of two witnesses at city hall. But you have many more options. Non-religious ceremonies can be just as special as religious ceremonies because they're about the couple itself and the bonds of love that link all the guests. Consider a ceremony that uses the cultural aspects of your background, rather than the religious. David Vallee knows of a rabbi who will perform a Jewish ceremony that involves all the traditions, like stomping on a glass, but makes no mention of God.

Religious ceremonies are still popular because they are imbued with centuries of tradition and meaning, so you may feel more comfortable going that route, regardless of how often your shadows darken the doorstep of a temple or church. Couples often opt for a religious ceremony even if they aren't religious, either because their parents insist on it (there they go again!) or that's just the way they always imagined their wedding day. If you do want to get married in a place of worship, but neither of you regularly attends, you'll probably be a little freaked out by the thought of having to choose unfamiliar readings and rituals. Rely on your officiant to guide you. He or she can let you know what options you have and what will suit your style as a couple.

Give your ceremony the careful thought it deserves. After all, it is your convenient excuse for throwing the big, crazy bash that follows.

♣ Multiculture, Megabucks

In this age of multicultural and interfaith marriages, deciding on whose culture or religion will be reflected in your ceremony can be a real minefield. Even if the two of you easily come to a decision, you're not getting married in a vacuum. Your parents may feel very differently, especially if they're helping pay for it. However, don't completely

suppress your own wishes. You have options, says David, and you can probably negotiate a middle path.

One path a lot of interfaith couples take is to have two ceremonies. Often one family will pay for one of the ceremonies in order to help their dream for your day happen. That's a great option if you have that kind of support, but if you do decide on two ceremonies, consider hiring a wedding planner. Planning two weddings is a massive amount of work for two people who probably already have full-time jobs. Many wedding planners specialize in cultural weddings, or are at least familiar with the customs.

If you decide to have just one ceremony, try to incorporate traditions from both cultures. Your officiant will probably respect the fact that we live in a multicultural society, and allow you to customize the ceremony, such as inviting an officiant of a different faith to participate. Another option is to avoid the issue entirely and have a civil ceremony at the reception venue. Your parents might howl, but try

Almost there! Just two little words, and it'll be happily ever after.

Michelle & Peter
The stress of planning melted away when it came time for Michelle and Peter to exchange vows.

Natalie & Blair
An elated Blair jumped the gun and tried to kiss his shocked bride without the minister's go-ahead.

to convince them that it is the best way to show your respect for all the guests. Everyone will be equally comfortable (or uncomfortable), and no one will feel left out.

❧ Your "I Do" Venue

In North America, it's still pretty common to get married in the bride's place of worship. If this suits you just fine, your choice is easy. Just make sure you book early to get your date. If you don't belong to a congregation, but have a particular place in mind, book even earlier, like more than a year in advance. The most spectacular churches and temples fill up fast. But there are endless options for where you can get married. If you want a religious ceremony outside of a place of worship, make sure the officiant will perform the ceremony. If it's a civil ceremony, you can get married anywhere that parking, city permits, or your budget allows. **The most affordable option is to have your ceremony and reception in the same venue.** But your choices for ceremony venues are endless. If you get married outside, have a back-up plan for bad weather. If you get married underwater, find an officiant who can swim.

A wedding is no place for quiet solemnity. It's a celebration, so enjoy your ceremony!

✤ Master or Mistress of the Ceremony

Whatever ceremony you choose to have, your officiant will let you know what your options are. Religious officiants and venues definitely make you play it their way. They should tell you what music is allowed and what isn't, if there are any limitations on photography and decoration, and if there are any restrictions on what you can wear. Some won't allow your photographer to be at the front of the venue during the ceremony. Which could be a blessing: Do you really want your grand entrance preceded by a photographer stumbling backward up the aisle? Some venues won't allow candelabras due to the fire hazard, or flowers on the altar, or tape or tacks on the walls and seating. Incredibly, they may also have restrictions about whom they will marry: If either of you is divorced, or of a different faith than that of the officiant, or, say, pregnant, there's a chance you might have to find someone a bit more open-minded.

Non-religious officiants usually don't care what you'll be wearing or who else you've been married to. In these cases, it's important to check with the venue for things that could trip up your ceremony. It should let you know what kind of sound system it'll provide, whether you'll be microphoned, and when you can have a rehearsal. Ask if any other ceremonies will be performed that day, since it could affect the time you get married and when you can decorate. Hopefully you'll be the only one, so you can

DAVID VALLEE ON SCREENING YOUR OFFICIANT: *Not all religious officiants are thrilled about performing weddings, especially if you're not in their congregation. Ask point blank if they enjoy performing marriages. If they hesitate, find another one. Unless, of course, you're entertained by the idea of a distracted priest administering your sacred vows.*

decorate after the rehearsal or the morning of the wedding. And so you won't be rushed out the door as soon as you say "I do."

A good officiant can induce tears or laughter; a bad officiant can induce yawns or groans. Although a monotonous or muddled officiant is great fodder for an unforgettable wedding video, an intentionally funny one is actually an asset. He or she can help loosen you up and make you feel comfortable so that you actually communicate with

Don't trust the all-important rings to just anyone. Delegate
attendants who will have them at the ready.

each other during the vows, rather than staring at each other in abject fear. Just be sure to ask what will be talked about in the address or homily, or if you can see it in advance. If you have no interest in having children, the last thing you want is for your rabbi to go on for ten minutes about how the whole point of marriage is procreation.

❀ Vows that Wow

The officiant should let you know how often he'll meet with you, and will probably give you options to go over on your own. Spend some time together picking vows, readings, and songs that reflect you. Your ceremony should be a joyful and touching tribute to your relationship and to who you are as individuals. The little things that you put into it make all the difference for your guests. Naturally, the vows are the most important part. What you say to each other at that moment is meant to represent everything you feel for each other and every way you promise to love each other for the rest of your lives. So you might want to spend some time on the vows. Writing your own is the most personal way to do this, but it can be a little overwhelming. If you're struggling for the right words, it's perfectly fine to seek outside help. Just type "wedding vows" into an Internet search engine and you'll find thousands of ideas to inspire you. And no one needs to know.

Or you could consider traditional vows. They're popular for a reason: They're replete with history, they say everything you want to say, and they do it beautifully. But they're not exactly timeless. Your officiant will give you various vows to choose from, and will probably let you make some minor—but important—changes. After all, you don't want to be caught saying something you have no intention of following through on. For instance, do you honestly feel like vowing to "obey" your husband? And why is it always the bride who vows to obey, and never the groom? Same goes for other aspects of the ceremony. You may not be comfortable with the idea of being "given away" by your father. Nobody owns you! Rest assured that you can often change it so that your family can "support your marriage" instead. Officiants will happily provide you with enough alternatives for you both to find something you're comfortable with.

Readings can be a particularly unique part of your wedding, and you can draw on all sorts of sources for them. Kahlil Gibran, Elizabeth Barrett Browning, and Corinthians are perennial favorites, but your readings should reflect you as a couple, so use anything and everything—rock song lyrics, movie lines, quotes from *The Simpsons*—for inspira-

Nancy & Fred
married: 25 years
wedding budget:
$8,000

The minister of the church turned out to be a doctor of divinity who had failed me in high school in religious knowledge.

And we were also living together at the time, so two knocks against us!

tion. Think seriously about the people you want giving the readings. As short as a reading is, one delivered in a monotone or with lots of mispronounced words (like, say, "Kahlil Gibran") will turn your perfect ceremony into a YouTube clip. Pick people who you know will be serious about it, who won't be speaking in public for the first time, or who mean a lot to the two of you but didn't make the wedding-party cut. Then give them readings ahead of time so they can practice. And when you're overwhelmed with all these choices, make sure you set aside some time to work on one of the most important parts of the ceremony—the kiss.

❧ Avoiding the Hollywood Marriage

Many officiants will suggest, or even require, that you attend marriage courses or pre-marriage counseling. They may provide this service themselves, it may be offered in

the place of worship, or they may suggest a third-party provider. Go ahead, roll your eyes and groan. But don't ignore their suggestion. Marriage courses can be fun! And honestly, you could probably use the help. You may think you know what you're getting into, but you don't. If you're living together already, you may envision marriage as the same old drill. But you probably have expectations of each other that you may not even have acknowledged, so you need to get those out in the open. Classes range in length from one night to a weekend to one night a week for a few months.

❧ Forever Ain't Free

Expect a religious ceremony to cost around $1,000. This includes the officiant's honorarium and a fee for clean-up. It will include rental of the place of worship if neither of you is a member of the congregation, and may include

When the pressures of planning get to you,
imagine the moment that will make it all worthwhile.

the services of the organist. A civil ceremony usually costs a couple hundred dollars, not including the venue fee, which you can reduce by having the ceremony at your reception venue. **A cocktail ceremony is a great way to save time and money, especially if you have it on a Friday evening. You eliminate the two-part, all-day wedding by having the ceremony and reception simultaneously.** Start cocktails before your ceremony, and when it's time to get married, gather everyone around, drinks in hand. Just make sure your officiant will perform the ceremony under these conditions. She may not be thrilled when you hand her a cocktail and say, "Let's get this thing over with!"

A ceremony can happen almost anywhere, provided you find an officiant who agrees. Why not pick a place that inspires you?

Novel Venues for Uncommon Couples

Don't feel tied to the classic temple-and-hall combo. Your wedding—both the ceremony and the reception—can happen anywhere you can imagine. Here's a list to get you started.

1 A **café** in a historic building with high ceilings can make for a stunning yet intimate affair. Think *fin-de-siècle* Paris...or turn-of-the-millennium *Friends*.

2 Like beer? Who doesn't! **Microbreweries** are often housed in historic or unique buildings that can be rented out. And you'll be hard pressed to run out of beverages.

3 The rustic, cavernous setting of a **market** makes a really unique venue and is something your guests are bound to talk about years from now. Even fish markets have housed grand affairs—following the effective application of a high-powered pressure washer.

4 **Museums and art galleries** are well-equipped for your über-cultural wedding. Dance under the dinosaurs, or toast amid the Tintorettos.

5 **Yachts** can often be hired for weddings of any size. But the *Love Boat* this ain't—the captain can't do the honors, so bring your own officiant.

6 A **beach** is a gorgeous setting for a barefoot wedding, and it doesn't have to be tropical. A local beach will do, provided you can be assured of some privacy. The last thing you want during your ceremony is for your guests to be distracted by the sight of some old guy in a Speedo.

7 Think "in the spotlight" isn't just a figure of speech? For a dramatic wedding, rent the lobby of a **theater**—or even the stage.

8 A **wine cellar** can make a small wedding cozy and elegant at the same time. Provided you're not claustrophobic.

9 **Historical buildings** can usually be rented for events—whether the lobby of a library or courthouse, the auditorium in an old town hall, or the chapel and saloon in a pioneer village.

10 **Barns** aren't just for cattle. They're also for barn dances! If you have access to a large barn, you've got enough space for a home-style—or ironically formal—country wedding.

THE RECEPTION: *It's All Relative*

The deed is done, you've gone down the aisle, and you're out the door. Now the party can start! But first, what do your guests do while you're off having your photos taken? Better take care of them, say Chantel and Charmaine, and don't keep them waiting too long.

If your ceremony and reception are at the same site, the wait should be no more than two hours, since many guests probably won't have the option of going home. (You know it's been too long when people are leaning against trees and running out of conversation.) One way to accommodate your guests is to include them in your photo shoot to some degree.

Chantel and Charmaine planned one wedding where the couple had their pictures taken on a beach. They invited their guests, gave them something to eat, and had a steel pan band perform. If you're going to invite your guests, though, give them something to do

> **CHANTEL AND CHARMAINE ON LONG WAITS:** *You can't avoid a long period of time between the ceremony and the reception if your religion or culture requires that you get married before noon. Don't leave your guests entirely on their own. Serve lunch after the ceremony, and give suggestions for activities they can do over the next few hours.*

so they're not interfering while your photographer tries to do his or her job. Have entertainment, put out the guestbook, set up photos of the two of you for them to look at, and serve cocktails and hors d'oeuvres. Keep 'em fed and distracted, and the time will fly.

❧ Pressing the Flesh

It may make sense to have a receiving line after the ceremony. You walk down the aisle, people follow you, and you stop and shake their hands on the way out. Then, when everybody's outside, you appear on the steps, are showered with bubbles or birdseed, and your guests get the perfect photo op. Sometimes, instead of a receiving line, the couple will walk around the reception handing out favors in order to say hi to everyone. But traditionally, the receiving line is done before the reception, and consists of the bride and groom and their parents. Depending on your culture—or how early you want to get the party started—you can have the groomsmen serve each guest a shot of liquor as they go through the receiving line. Now that's worth lining up for!

Once you've got your guests into your reception, where do they go? Give them lots of clues. You can list the seating arrangements on an easel, or you can have someone sitting at a table at the entrance telling them where to sit. Chantel and Charmaine recommend you provide both. Some people like to ask for help, and some like to find their own way, so cater to both groups. This will also help cut down on congestion. A lot of couples have fun with seating arrangements,

using names or pictures that match their theme or interests, rather than numbers. The seating chart, like everything else, should fit the décor, and it should be big enough for senior citizens to read.

Seating cards are another option, and a table full of tented cards can look very formal, but the cards can also be a pain in the neck. The idea is that a card is printed for each guest with his or her seating assignment on the back. The cards are laid out on a table at the entrance in alphabetical order. Guests find their cards, pick them up, and go to their tables. If your wedding is formal, you'll probably want to do this, but if it's not, it's not worth the bother of extra stationery expenses, misplaced cards, and a domino effect when the air conditioning blasts.

Your guests can't be expected to entertain themselves once you've left the ceremony to have pictures taken. Provide cocktails and other distractions to make the time fly.

Sneaking in the side door is not an option. Your entrance
should be an event.

🌹 Making an Entrance

The grand entrance is your chance to shine. It can also be ridiculously expensive. If you have the budget, you can have fireworks, a hot air balloon, a helicopter…anything that the reception venue can accommodate. If you don't have the funds, bring it back to the theme of your wedding, and make it something that reflects you. Chantel and Charmaine have planned a couple of weddings where the entrances were both spectacular and deeply personal. At an African wedding, a crowd of the couple's relatives entered the room dressed in colorful garments, singing in their native tongue and dancing, with the couple hidden in the middle. It was a huge thrill for the guests, and very personal for the bride and groom. Another dazzling entrance arranged by Chantel and Charmaine was led by a Chinese dragon.

Having members of your family usher you into the room in a dramatic way is not only very special, it's also affordable. If your budget doesn't allow for a light show worthy of the opening ceremonies of the Olympics, be creative. In a wedding that Heidi planned, the couple couldn't afford the fireworks they had hoped for, so Heidi found a high-school drum line to perform as they walked in. The combination of the surprise—it was something no one had seen before, and Heidi had managed to sneak the drummers into the building—the fact that it

An extravagant set of wheels is only worth it if your guests get to see it.

seemed a natural fit for the couple, a teacher and a police officer, and the sheer spectacle really impressed the guests. However, just because you can afford a helicopter entrance doesn't mean you should do it. A successful entrance involves the guests, rather than being something they have to go out of their way to see. Dragging everyone out of their seats to look out the window, or outside so that they have to dispose of their drinks, is not going to impress them, no matter how extraordinary the mode of transportation.

The simplest way to enter the room is to have the emcee announce you. Some couples decide to do the first dance as soon as they enter. It does work as a natural progression from the announcement, and it gets the dance out of the way, so you don't have to try to remember your steps all through dinner. Or, if you've booked your photographer for only a few hours, it ensures you get a picture of the dance. It also means

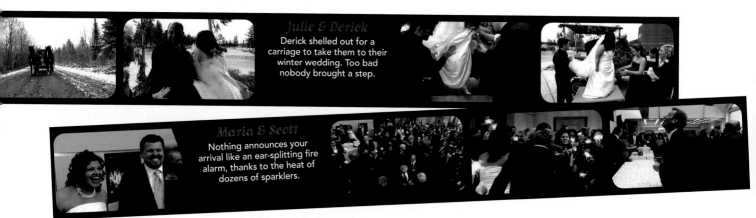

Julie & Derick
Derick shelled out for a carriage to take them to their winter wedding. Too bad nobody brought a step.

Maria & Scott
Nothing announces your arrival like an ear-splitting fire alarm, thanks to the heat of dozens of sparklers.

that everyone else gets to see it, including your elderly grandparents, who may run out of steam and head home as soon as they've finished eating. If you're self-conscious, or not exactly a born dancer, just turn down the lights. Your guests won't notice that you're stepping on each other's feet as long as the lights are low.

🌹 Leading the Proceedings

Your emcee will be the life of the party, so choose wisely. Bad emcees are monotonous; really bad emcees are offensive. Either one will bring down your party. A good emcee doesn't have to be wildly entertaining, but he or she has to be lively and must be able to relate to the crowd. If you don't have a close friend or relative whom you can rely on to get the party going, don't pick just anyone that's close to you. That uncle who has you in stitches at Thanksgiving dinner may suddenly become mute when faced with a hall full of people. It's important to know whether the person is going to be comfortable and full of energy when the time comes. If no one fits the bill, and you're thinking of asking your frat brother but you're not sure whether he can resist telling the story of how you lost your virginity, consider hiring a professional instead. Many DJs will provide a professional emcee for a few hundred dollars.

Get your first dance over
with when you arrive,
or use it to lead the crush
to the dance floor.

🌹 Let's Eat!

Finally, the moment they've been waiting for since they woke up this morning. Now that your guests are at the table, any amount of time they have to wait for dinner will be unduly frustrating. Sure, they should be chatting with the people at their table, making new friends and reacquainting with old, but they're also completely fixated on when their food will arrive or when they'll get to go up to the buffet. The need for speed in serving the meal is one of the reasons why it's important not to pick apart the catering quote. For a buffet, have at least two lines and have enough serving staff to keep the lines moving. The last thing you want is for half the room to have finished eating while the other half is still waiting to line up. Just in case the food is slow to come, keep up the energy in the room with music and entertainment. Chantel and Charmaine suggest having a contest where the table that waits the longest gets a prize, such as restaurant gift certificates. This will keep your guests' interest up, and they'll actually be excited to be the last table called.

Dessert and toasts often coincide—although they don't have to—because time is running short and those people who don't want to stick around to dance are getting ready to leave. It's best not to let the toasts, the slideshow, and your thank-yous go on too long. As important as the bride and groom's thank you speech and first dance are, they often become emotional. While emotion is great, it's probably going to bring your party down a bit. Keep it short, then hit them with something spectacular.

Martha & Steve
married: 45 years
wedding budget: $1,500

There was one drunk uncle, and he wanted to dance with me, and he said he'd give me $20 if he could dance with me.

That started a chain, so Martha was making money for us to help pay for our honeymoon.

❧ Dance the Night Away

Chantel and Charmaine suggest you bring out your best entertainment right after dinner. The bouquet throwing and garter toss, if you opt for them (and you *so* don't have to), can wait until later, when the guests who will participate

Force the crowd onto their feet as soon as possible so reluctant guests aren't tempted to head home early.

Know Thy DJ

Have some idea of what your DJ might make you do for the sake of entertaining your guests. If you want to stay low-key, a band might be better.

in them make up a greater portion of the guests still there, unless you've chosen to give your bouquet to an honored guest, such as the oldest couple or a same-sex couple who can't get married. Otherwise, these hallowed traditions are often a signal that the bride

> **DAVID VALLEE ON THE TOAST WITH THE MOST:** *Four speeches is optimum: the parents, a friend of the bride, and a friend of the groom. Toasts should last less than two minutes, and they should be given from notes, not written out verbatim. The speakers should tell one anecdote that encapsulates your relationship, raise their glass, and sit down.*

and groom are about to call it a night. Having the groom crawl up the bride's dress to fetch the garter with his teeth has to be a prelude to something, after all.

Begin the dance with something that will bring everyone out onto the floor. A DJ will have some ideas, but an ethnic dance is a great start. Have the dancers coax guests up to get everyone involved, then the DJ or band can slowly take over. Or ask the DJ or band to start with music for the older guests. If you play young music right away, the older adults won't dance and will probably just go home. Beyoncé can wait. But don't worry. Younger guests will probably recognize their parents' music, so before you know it, the dance floor will be hopping.

Save the best for last: Bouquet and garter tosses are a signal that you're passing the torch and heading off on your honeymoon.

The Kiss: Making Them Work for the Money Shot

The clinking of cutlery on glass is a sound seldom heard in today's weddings. Good riddance. Guests have to work a lot harder to get the couple to kiss, and couples are very inventive in what they're making guests do:

1 **Asking tables to sing a song with the word "love" in it is a popular choice among couples.** Your group of friends has probably sung "Love, Love Me Do" or "I Was Made for Loving You" at several weddings by now, though, so the thrill may be gone.

2 **A guest spins the wheel, and if it lands on a gold star, the bride and groom kiss.** Every other space has an activity the guest must do, such as sing a TV theme song, do the moonwalk, kiss his neighbor, or order drinks for his table.

3 Print questions about the bride and groom on slips of paper and stick them in balloons. **Guests must pop a balloon, and if they answer the question correctly, the bride and groom kiss.**

4 Get your guests out of their seats. **A hole-in-one contest is a popular choice.**

5 Have guests make a donation to a charity. No coins, please!

6 **Have someone hide Hershey's Kisses around the room. If a guest finds a Kiss, they can present it to the bride and groom to make them kiss.** This requires CIA-level security, though. Make sure no one finds out in time to bring their own kisses, and pick someone who won't be participating to hide them.

7 Ask guests to **tell a story about the bride or groom**, or to give them advice for their marriage.

8 Lots of DJs can bring giant dice that have pictures of lips on a couple of sides. **Guests rolls the die, and if they get the lips, the bride and groom kiss.** If they get a number instead, they have to kiss that number of people.

9 **Invite older couples up to "show you how it's done."** You'd be surprised how daring those senior citizens can be.

10 But if you just want to enjoy your meal without all that standing up and sitting down, some activities can reduce the amount of kissing you'll have to do. **If the activity is too embarrassing (like, say, riding a tricycle) or challenging (riding a tricycle in formal wear), your problem is solved.**

Your PERFECT DAY

The planning's complete, and there's no turning back. Congratulations on making it this far

with your sanity intact! Now, as the deadline looms, it's time to focus on those last-minute

details. Does everyone know where they need to be and when? Are your vendors going

to show up on time and with exactly what you ordered? Why can't you shake that nagging

feeling that you've overlooked something? Just follow this schedule, and you won't be the

bride who forgot to pick up her wedding dress or the groom who forgot the rings.

❊ The Final Countdown: The Last Two Weeks

Remember all those vendors who were so enthusiastic about your wedding four months ago? They've probably done a whack of weddings since, so now is a good time to say hi and make sure you're still on their radar. Call them to confirm the details, give final numbers, and make your last payments. (Of course, if you've hired a wedding planner, this will be taken care of for you.) Contact everyone who has agreed to help out, especially your attendants, and send them an itinerary for the wedding day. Your attendants have probably been devoting lots of time to your shower and bachelor party, so devote some attention to them in return. Make sure they've confirmed tux rentals or that their alterations are finished. The bridesmaids should be picking up their dresses and shoes. The wedding dress should also be ready, but don't pick it up yet—leave that until the last week. If you bring it home early, it can pick up the cooking smells in your home, become wrinkled or crushed, or fall prey to your niece's magic-marker embellishments.

Chantel & Scott
Chantel's dream for her cake made David cringe. Fortunately, Chantel saw that simpler could definitely be better.

❊ Vow to Start Early

If you're writing your own vows, and you haven't started them by now, get on it. A lot of brides imagine this scenario: They're soaking in a candlelit tub on the night before their wedding, writing their vows while soft music plays in the background, and in the serenity of the moment it all just comes to them. The reality is, even if you're not rushing to finish the favors or drinking too much wine at the rehearsal dinner, you both have so many things running through your heads that you won't be able to focus, and the vows won't be sincere. This is your chance to articulate in public how you feel about your soon-to-be spouse, while you have everyone's attention. So start early, write down anything that inspires you, and work hard.

The same goes for your thank-you speech. Once the best man and the maid of honor have voiced touching tributes to your friendship, it will be time for the two of you to take the mike and thank your family for their support and hard work, the vendors for their skill and profession-alism, and your friends for coming out and making it a great party. It's not the end of the world if you end up winging it, but if you write it ahead of time, you won't

With so many things to do in the last couple weeks, an organized bride won't forget the things that really count.

forget to thank your hard-working wedding party; or Cousin Phil, who came all the way from South Korea; or the caterer, who might be waiting in the kitchen door for his or her acknowledgment.

❋ The Seating Dance

Until you know who is coming to your wedding, working on the seating arrangement will be an exercise in futility. Plan to give yourselves plenty of time for this in the last couple of weeks. A great deal of finesse and foresight is required to negotiate divorces, fallen-out friends, and awkward numbers. Get a head start by trying to slot people into place as the replies come in, and by following up with any guests you haven't heard from. It's best to do the seating plan yourselves, with no input from friends and relatives who have their own opinions, but if you're feeling overwhelmed, you can hand different parts of the guest list off to your parents and close friends who understand the dynamics of the different groups. If you don't want to be the ones to decide which estranged relatives should be stuck together, claim you have too much to do and stick someone else with it.

Take time to tell your friends how much you appreciate their help. They're spending the entire day in heels for you, after all.

Make a checklist of all the little things that can get lost when you're just looking at the big picture, like the guestbook, a unity candle, or accessories for your outfits. This is not the time to be hit by inspiration, however. A lot of couples panic at this point because it's their last chance to plan the wedding—their last chance to make it perfect—and they end up blowing their budget in the final hour. So put that sudden need for a photo booth in perspective. It's probably not as important or impressive as you think it is, you probably can't afford it by now, and any other distractions you add will just overwhelm your guests. If you have a cohesive theme or vision for the wedding, you're less likely to be caught up in last-minute must-haves.

❋ Last Week, Last Chance

If you can spare the vacation time and you haven't hired a wedding planner, or you have lots of family coming in from out of town, it's a good idea to take the last few days off. If everything's in order or the wedding planner is on the job, you probably

> **CHANTEL AND CHARMAINE ON DATE NIGHT:** *The week before your wedding, spend a nice evening together talking about anything but. Often the stress of the last few weeks causes arguments and tension. It's really important to take some time to regroup, reconnect, and remember the point of all the chaos.*

only need to take the day before off. Start packing for the honeymoon early in the week. Take an evening to make a list, do your laundry, and pack everything you can. So many couples leave it to the last minute and end up at a resort without a bathing suit. Pack a bag for the wedding night, too—something almost everyone forgets to do! Leaving the hotel in a rumpled tux the day after your wedding isn't the classiest way to start your honeymoon.

❋ Getting It Right

The wedding rehearsal is the key to a smooth ceremony, although you won't be able to tell from the gaggle of groomsmen goofing off in the back of the room. It's usually held a day or two before the wedding day (your ceremony venue should let you know what times are available). Even though it's important to you, strangely enough the rehearsal is not a priority for your wedding party. Most people will show up late, so tell them to be there 15 minutes before you actually want them there—a good idea for the wedding day, too!

You may not absorb a lot of information during the rehearsal, but don't worry, you're not expected to. The idea is to get a rough indication of what will happen and

to avoid surprises at the main event, so it's important to make sure everyone is paying at least some attention. For your attendants, rehearsals are often a necessary evil to be suffered through while waiting for the party that comes afterward. A wedding planner is a valuable ally to have at this point: to take charge, so the bride isn't screaming at her distracted friends; to make it fun, so it's actually interesting to the participants; and to make it quick, so everyone can get on to the best part.

Practice Makes Perfect

Pay attention during the rehearsal—as much as you can, anyway—and you'll be laughing all the way to the reception.

The only things you should really have to worry about
now are the most minor details.

Loribeth & Charisma

Their budget was a mystery—
the rest was easy. With Karina's help,
Loribeth and Charisma's wedding
day made everyone happy.

A good officiant or a patient bride and groom can also make it easier on everyone. Channel that crazy energy into making it a race down the aisle or a contest to see who can get it right the first time. Some couples opt to have the dinner before the rehearsal so that people aren't distracted by what comes next. Of course, rehearsals can be stressful in other ways too. Be prepared for the emotions it brings up for your parents. The father of the bride may suddenly decide it's time to take charge, or divorced parents may

ALLISTER ON WINING AND DINING YOUR WEDDING PARTY:

Often the rehearsal dinner is at a house or restaurant. You don't have to spend a fortune. We've done catered barbecues at home, and we've gone to restaurants that had private rooms and prix fixe meals. A day or two before your wedding, you shouldn't have to work.

become antagonistic when faced with the significance of what their child is about to do. Asking them (politely) to consider your current mental state might help them put aside any differences for now.

In an ideal world you won't have too much to do the day before. If you can drop off things like favors, the seating chart, and any other miscellaneous items at the reception venue ahead of time, get that out of the way now. Make sure the wedding dress and tuxes have been picked up. The bride should get a manicure and pedicure, and hey, so should the groom. And just to be sure you can get that all-important beauty sleep, review your checklists and itinerary one last night to make sure everything's done. Nothing helps you feel relaxed and confident more than knowing you've got it under control.

❋ Ready or Not...

The day has arrived, and if you've followed the *Rich Bride Poor Bride* planners' advice, you'll be spending it in style: playing golf, being pampered, sipping champagne, and relaxing with your friends. There are just a couple of things left to do before you walk down that aisle. First of all, make sure your attendants are where they have to be, that they have everything they need, and that they're not feeling left out. The whole reason for a wedding party is to have help at the ready on your wedding day, so take advantage of your supporting cast, but make sure they're pampered too. And most of all, remember to enjoy yourselves and each other. It's easy to get so caught up in the details that you miss your own party.

Your wedding day will be a party from start to finish, after all. The house will be full of people and full of energy. There will be food and music and laughter as your parents hover anxiously and your friends tease each other about their stylin' duds. Later on, you'll enter a room full of people who love you, all of them smiling at you and radiating warmth and best wishes. And even later, you'll find yourselves in the middle of the dance floor, with those same people surrounding you and having the time of their lives. Take several moments to bask in what you've created. It will fly by faster than you think.

After all the careful planning and finger-crossing, something will go wrong. Time and again on *Rich Bride Poor Bride*, small disasters happen: the door of the church

Jennifer & Charles
married: 21 years
wedding budget:
$5,000

Driving on our way home, we got all romantic. You know, we started to say little nice things to each other, and we're still saying them after all this time. And we also had a very good night at the Holiday Inn.

is locked, the favors were forgotten at home, the officiant is stuck in traffic. Big disasters can also happen. Your tent could leak on what was supposed to be the driest day of the year, forcing everyone inside the house, where a hundred pairs of muddy feet will destroy your parents' carpets. The happiest brides and grooms just take these things in stride. After all, you're married, enjoying fabulous food and music, and surrounded by people who love you, no matter where it happens or what your hair looks like. As the many *Rich Bride Poor Bride* couples attest at the end of each show, it doesn't get any better than that. Our wedding planners wish you the happiest, craziest, most beautiful day ever, whatever form fate decides that day will take.

Time to celebrate the fact that you got hitched . . . and it all went off without a hitch. Now the sparks can really fly!

Words of Wisdom for Your Wedding Day

When the day finally comes, the **Rich Bride Poor Bride** *planners want you to relax, enjoy, and remember why you're there. Here are their words of wisdom:*

1 Don't expect perfection for your wedding day. Expect a terrific day and set reasonable expectations. **Never forget the main goal is to get married.** Everything else is just icing on the cake.

2 On this same day around our wonderful, crazy world, kids will be born, someone will get bad news, and someone will get good news. **Keep this day in perspective.** It doesn't have to be "the happiest day of your life," but rather one of many magical days as you start your journey together as a couple.

3 **It is a day to celebrate your family and friends.** It is a time to write a hand-written note to your best friend from fifth grade who is still there for you, or do something incredible for your new in-laws during the reception, or celebrate your grandparents' marriages.

4 **Manage your expectations and be prepared for a snag or two in the road.** Just like marriage itself, wedding days take their own course. If something doesn't happen exactly as planned, roll with it. Don't let it ruin the day.

5 Believe in your choice. It sounds clichéd, but it is sometimes forgotten. **Regardless of your specific faith, you must believe in yourself, your partner, and your decisions.**

6 **Trust your day in the hands of others.** You should have a system in place that will allow you to let go of all your worries on your wedding day. You are the guests of honor; your biggest worry should be what number SPF to wear on your honeymoon.

7 Take a moment to breathe, look around you, and **enjoy what you have created.**

8 **Dance!** Or celebrate in whatever way suits you, but remember that this day is a celebration.

9 Go on a honeymoon. **You'll need some calm, uninterrupted time together to relax, get to know each other again, and forget about the craziness.** You've probably had enough of your family by now—and vice versa, likely—so use this time to get away.

10 When you return, you'll be just another married couple to the rest of the world. **Avoid the inevitable letdown by getting excited about the future.** Make a wedding scrapbook, plan a vacation, or decorate your home—your options are endless.

Contact Our Planners

Angelique's Weddings and Events

Angelique and her staff can provide wedding day coordination, or they can plan your entire wedding. They also plan destination weddings, showers, stag-and-doe parties, and corporate events.

Angelique Sobschak
www.angeliquesweddings.com
905-937-0355 or 1-866-682-9270
angelique@
angeliquesweddings.com

David Vallee Entertains

David Vallee and his team provide full-service catering and event planning, specializing in stylish, urban events.

David Vallee
www.dventertains.ca
416-364-2495
dvallee@dventertains.ca

theideashop

David and his business partner Jann Coppen specialize in event entertainment production. They plan and produce a wide range of private, corporate, and community events.

David Connolly
www.theideashop.ca
416-504-IDEA (4332)
info@theideashop.ca

Platinum Desk Concierge Service

Platinum Desk's concierge team handles event planning, personal shopping, gift shopping, home staging, interior design, and clutter management.

Allister Reid
www.platinumdesk.com
416-409-7858
platinumdesk1@aol.com

Posies Flower Shop

Posies specializes in contemporary, garden-inspired floral arrangements. Karina is an experienced wedding and event planner as well as a floral designer, and can help plan your entire wedding or make sure things run smoothly on the wedding day.

Karina Lemke
www.posiesflowers.com
416-588-9061
karina@posiesflowers.com

Prestige Image Consultants

Prestige Image Consultants can help you plan your wedding, but they also provide wardrobe, beauty pageant, and image consultations, personal shopping services, and seminars on social and business etiquette.

Ann-Marie Daniel-Barker
www.prestigeimage.ca
905-780-9500 or 416-697-9898
events@prestigeimage.ca

R&R Wedding and Event Designs

Chantel and Charmaine will plan every aspect of your wedding day, they'll deal with vendors on your behalf, they'll coordinate your wedding day, or they'll provide whatever amount of help you need.

Chantel Walker and
Charmaine Burke
www.rnrdesigns.ca
416-220-4442
info@rnrdesigns.ca

Weddings Heidi Style

Weddings Heidi Style is a bridal salon and wedding magazine, but Heidi is also an event planner, an image consultant, and a wedding photographer.

Heidi Allen
www.weddingsheidistyle.com
905-682-9191
heidi@weddingsheidistyle.com

Photo Resources

Azure Blue Photography

Stacey Barry

Something borrowed,
something blue

www.azureblue.ca

Christina Woerns
Photography

Christina Woerns

Christinawoernsphotography.
com

Christopher Gentile
Photography

Christopher Gentile
(Cover photography
& lead photographer)

www.christophergentile.ca

Concord Photography

Vladimir Bekker

www.concord-photo.com

Davide Greene
Photographer, LLC

Davide Greene

Working with couples in love
is my passion

www.idavide.com

Dawn Alexander
Photography

Dawn Alexander

www.dawnalexander.com

Gaffney Photo

Pete Gaffney

www.gaffneyphoto.com

HRM Photography

Heather MacEachern
& Lindsay Windebank

*We believe that each wedding
is as unique as the couple
who plans the occasion—
our photography reflects this*

www.hrmphotography.com

Ian Taylor Photography

Ian Taylor

*Taking a documentary approach
to wedding photography*

www.iantaylor.ca

Images by Van Dam

Mark Van Dam

*Award-Winning Wedding
Photography by Mark van Dam,
B.A., M.A.*

www.imagesbyvandam.com

Jean Heguy Photography

Jean Heguy

www.jeanheguy.com

**Joseph Vetrone
Photography**

Joseph Vetrone

*Fusing together the grandeur
of tradition and the poignancy
of emotion*

www.vetronephoto.com

**Reportage Event
Photography**

www.reportagephoto.com

**Richard Emmanuel
Studios of photography
& cinematography**

Richard Emmanuel

World's best photographers

www.richardemmanuel.com

Shooter4hire Photography

Paul Wright

Changing the way we look at photography

www.shooter4hire.com

Timevision Photography Inc.

Eduardo Martins

www.timevisionphoto.ca

WEDO Photography & Video

Daniel Royers

Experience counts

www.wedo.ca

Additional Resources

Posies Flower Shop Inc.

www.posiesflowers.com

Inviting Elegance

Begin your dream of a perfect wedding day by first… Inviting Elegance

www.invitingelegance.ca

GeniusLoci Fine Flowers

www.Geniusloci.ca

The Jewel Case LTD.

www.thejewelcase.ca

Bella Invites

Couture Wedding Stationery

www.bellainvites.com

Rainbow Invitations & Gifts Inc.

rainbowinvitations@bellnet.ca

Ashley Jewellery Collection

The Look finds by Frida

The Cake Box

www.cakebox.ca

Photo Credits

Front cover: Christopher Gentile Photography

Page ii: Christopher Gentile Photography

Page iv: Gaffney Photo

Page x: Azure Blue Photography

Page 1: Gaffney Photo

Page 3: Christopher Gentile Photography

MEET THE PLANNERS

Page 4: Joseph Vetrone Photography

Page 5-7: Christopher Gentile Photography; Jean Heguy Photography

Chapter 1:
IN THE BEGINNING

Page 8: HRM Photography

Page 11: Spiria Fearon

Page 12: HRM Photography

Page 13: Images by Van Dam

Page 14: HRM Photography

Page 17: Reportage Event Photography

Page 18: (From left to right) Reportage Event Photography; HRM Photography; Azure Blue

Photography; Reportage Event Photography

Page 19: (From left to right) HRM Photography; HRM Photography; Richard Emmanuel Studios of photography & cinematography; Christopher Gentile Photography, Art Direction: Spiria Fearon

Page 20: HRM Photography

Page 21: HRM Photography

Chapter 2:
GET DOWN WITH YOUR BUDGET

Page 22: HRM Photography

Page 25: HRM Photography

Page 26: HRM Photography

Page 28: (Top Left) HRM Photography; (Bottom Right) HRM Photography

Page 31: Azure Blue Photography

Page 32: HRM Photography

Chapter 3:
VA-VA-VOOM YOUR VENUE

Page 34: Shooter4hire Photography

Page 37: Davide Greene Photographer, LLC.

Page 38: Ian Taylor Photography

Page 41: Jean Heguy Photography

Page 42: (Left) Azure Blue Photography; (Right) HRM Photography

Page 45: HRM Photography

Page 46: HRM Photography

Page 47: Shooter4hire Photography

Chapter 4:
ALL THINGS PAPER

Page 48: Reportage Event Photography

Page 51: Reportage Event Photography

Page 52: Azure Blue Photography

Page 53: Christopher Gentile Photography, Art Direction: Spiria Fearon

Page 54: Sean Buckley

Page 55: (Top Left) HRM Photography; (Bottom Right) Christopher Gentile Photography

Page 56: Shooter4hire Photography

Page 58: Jean Heguy Photography

Page 59: HRM Photography

Page 60: Reportage Event Photography

Page 61: Reportage Event Photography

Chapter 5:
DRESSES AND TRESSES

Page 62: Dawn Alexander Photography

Page 65: Ian Taylor Photography

Page 66: Concord Photography

Page 67: (Top Left) HRM Photography; (Bottom Right) Images by Van Dam

Page 68: Reportage Event Photography

Page 71: Richard Emmanuel Studios of photography & cinematography

Page 73: HRM Photography

Page 75: Timevision Photography Inc.

Page 76: Shooter4hire Photography

Page 77: (Top Left) HRM Photography; (Middle) HRM Photography; (Top Right) Concord

Photography; (Bottom Right) Azure Blue Photography; (Bottom Left) HRM Photography

Page 78: HRM Photography

Page 79: Gaffney Photo

Chapter 6:
THE TUX MANUAL

Page 80: Gaffney Photo

Page 83: Gord Seblefski

Page 84: HRM Photography

Page 85: Azure Blue Photography

Page 86: (Top Left) Shooter4hire Photography; (Middle Left) Christopher Gentile Photography; (Bottom Left) HRM Photography

Page 87: WEDO Photography & Video

Page 88: Reportage Event Photography

Page 89: HRM Photography

Chapter 7:
TO EAT IS DIVINE

Page 90: Christopher Gentile Photography, Art Direction: Spiria Fearon

Page 92: Christopher Gentile Photography, Art Direction: Spiria Fearon

Page 93: HRM Photography

Page 94: (Left) Reportage Event Photography; (Middle) Owen & Christine Hargreaves; (Bottom Right) Reportage Event Photography

Page 96: HRM Photography

Page 97: HRM Photography

Page 99: HRM Photography

Page 100: (Top Left) Christopher Gentile Photography, Art Direction: Spiria Fearon; (Middle Left) Christopher Gentile Photography, Art Direction: Spiria Fearon; (Bottom Left) Christopher Gentile Photography, Art Direction: Spiria Fearon; (Bottom) Christopher Gentile Photography, Art Direction: Spiria Fearon; (Right) Reportage Event Photography

Page 102: Azure Blue Photography

Page 103: Reportage Event Photography

Page 104: Christopher Gentile Photography, Art Direction: Spiria Fearon

Page 105: Reportage Event Photography

Chapter 8:
COMING UP ROSES

Page 106: Ian Taylor Photography

Page 108: HRM Photography

Page 109: HRM Photography

Page 110: Dawn Alexander Photography

Page 111: HRM Photography

Page 112: (Left) Azure Blue Photography; (Top) HRM Photography; (Right) HRM Photography; (Bottom Right) HRM Photography; (Bottom Left) HRM Photography

Page 113: HRM Photography

Page 114: HRM Photography

Page 117: Reportage Event Photography

Page 118: HRM Photography

Page 119: HRM Photography

Chapter 9:
SAY CHEESE (NOT CHEESY)

Page 120: WEDO Photography & Video

Page 123: Davide Greene Photographer, LLC.

Page 125: Richard Emmanuel Studios of photography & cinematography

Page 126: Shooter4hire Photography

Page 129: Timevision Photography Inc.

Page 131: HRM Photography

Page 132: Timevision Photography Inc.

Page 133: Ian Taylor Photography

Chapter 10:
ALL ABOUT HAR-MONEY

Page 134: Jean Heguy Photography

Page 137: HRM Photography

Page 138: Concord Photography

Page 141: Images by Van Dam

Page 143: Christina Woerns Photography

Page 144: HRM Photography

Page 145: (Upper Left) Reportage Event Photography; (Bottom Right) Dawn Alexander Photography

Page 146: Reportage Event Photography

National Library of Canada Cataloguing in Publication Data

Rich bride, poor bride : your ultimate wedding planning guide / Buck Productions.

Includes index.

ISBN 978-0-470-15446-5

    1. Weddings--Planning. 2. Wedding etiquette. I. Buck

Productions

HQ745.R53 2007   395.2'2   C2007-906406-X

Production Credits

Cover design: Ian Koo

Interior design: Amy Henderson

Interior photography: See photo credits

Interior photo-imaging: Jason Vandenberg

Typesetting: Amy Henderson

Front cover photo: Christopher Gentile

Back cover photo: Christopher Gentile

Printer: Friesens

John Wiley & Sons Canada, Ltd.

6045 Freemont Blvd.

Mississauga, Ontario

L5R 4J3

Printed in Canada

1 2 3 4 5 FP 11 10 09 08 07